# CHAINBREAKER'S
# WAR

Daguerreotype portrait of Chainbreaker in 1859. Reproduced in Thomas Donaldson, *Indians—the Six Nations of New York: Cayugas, Mohawks (St. Regis), Oneidas, Onondagas, Senecas, Tuscaroras,* Extra Census Bulletin (Washington, DC: U. S. Census Printing Office, 1892). Courtesy Gloversville Free Library.

# CHAINBREAKER'S WAR

*A Seneca Chief Remembers
the American Revolution*

An Authentic Narrative Edited by
Jeanne Winston Adler

BLACK · DOME

Black Dome Press Corp.
www.blackdomepress.com

Published by
Black Dome Press Corp.
1011 Route 296
Hensonville, New York 12439
www.blackdomepress.com
(518) 734-6357

First Edition

Library of Congress Cataloging-in-Publication Data

Blacksnake, Governor, ca. 1753-1859.
    Chainbreaker's war : a Seneca chief remembers the American Revolution / edited by
Jeanne Winston Adler.-- 1st ed.
       p. cm.
    Includes bibliographical references and index.
    ISBN 1-883789-33-8 (trade paper)
      1. Blacksnake, Governor, ca. 1753-1859. 2. Seneca Indians--Kings and
rulers--Biography. 3. Indians of North America--History--Revolution, 1775-1783. 4.
United States--History--Revolution, 1775-1783--Participation, Indian. 5. United
States--History--Revolution, 1775-1783--Personal narratives.  I. Adler, Jeanne Winston,
1946- II. Title.

E99.S3 B534 2002
973.3'092--dc21
[B]
                                                                        2002018599

Cover Painting: Detail from *Concealed Enemy*, oil painting, 1845, George C. Bingham. Collection of Stark Museum of Art, Orange, Texas.

Design by Carol Clement, Artemisia, Inc.

Printed in the USA

# Acknowledgments

This volume appears in print thanks to the contributions of an astonishingly long list of people. The list begins with Douglas Glover, who was kind enough to tell me about Chainbreaker's narrative in the first place. He had consulted it along with others of the Draper Manuscripts in researching his fictional account of the Revolutionary War in northern New York, *The Life and Times of Captain N.* Malcolm Jensen, then editor of Cobblestone Publishing of Peterborough, New Hampshire, encouraged me to transcribe and edit the narrative, which I accessed on microfilm in the New York State Library in Albany and in Lamont Library, Cambridge, Massachusetts. Though Malcolm ultimately judged the material wrong for Cobblestone, his personal enthusiasm for Chainbreaker's saga impelled me forward with the project. He also alerted me to Thomas Abler's 1989 study of the narrative, which helped to answer so many "who, what, why, where, when" questions about Chainbreaker's story. Librarians at the New York State Library, Crandall Library of Glens Falls, and Saratoga Springs Library assisted me in locating many of the "voices" that accompany Chainbreaker's here. I'm particularly grateful to the NYSL Newspaper Project, which enabled me to read "up-to-the-minute" news reports on the Senecas' 1792 visit to Philadelphia. Jane

Loeb and Anna Chapman of Cambridge Writers and Poets both read and edited my nearly complete manuscript, improving its flow through punctuation changes as well as offering other useful criticisms. Anna Chapman also prepared the index. Virginia Hurt assisted me in the search for a publisher, and Marie Jensen, sister of Malcolm, introduced me to Black Dome Press, at last. Debbie Allen and Steve Hoare of Black Dome gave my manuscript exceptionally fine treatment—with the help of designer Carol Clement and copyeditors Matina Billias, Erin Mulligan, and Ed Volmar. Mary Bogin of Onondaga Community College urged me to approach Peter Jemison for an introduction, and I am extremely grateful to both Mary and Peter for his wonderful essay and memoir. My father, Gordon R. Willey, supplied the book's preface, and my very special and loving thanks go to him.

Jeanne Winston Adler
Salem, NY
June, 2002

# Contents

*Preface*  9
Gordon R. Willey

*Foreword*  11
G. Peter Jemison

CHAINBREAKER SPEAKS  19

EDITOR'S NOTE  22

CHAPTER ONE  29
"No People Can Live More Happy"

CHAPTER TWO  48
"We Will Go and Attend the Father"

CHAPTER THREE  63
"Few White Men Escaped from Us"

CHAPTER FOUR  70
"It Was Done in Honor"

CHAPTER FIVE  81
"I Killed Many"

CHAPTER SIX   95
"The Danger Was Near at Hand"

CHAPTER SEVEN   130
"Remember Me Who Rescued You"

CHAPTER EIGHT   140
"We Won't Give Up Our Lands"

CHAPTER NINE   157
"The War Was Now Closed"

CHAPTER TEN   175
"They Gave Us Poison in Return"

CHAPTER ELEVEN   199
"To Go West Once More"

AFTERWORD   206

*Notes*   209

*Annotated Bibliography*   214

*Index*   220

# Preface

The American Indians, the native peoples who occupied the New World at the time of its fifteenth-century discovery, have always loomed large in the thinking of their European discoverers. These European, or "White Man's," thoughts about the Native American "Red Man" have varied from the fanciful to the down-to-earth, as well as to frequent condemnation mixed with occasional praise. Here in North America, during the last century-and-a-half, the Indian aborigines have been studied by archaeologists, ethnologists, linguists, and historians so that gradually both scholars and the general public have come to know more about them.

One such group of the American Indians that has attracted particular attention has been the Iroquois who had long occupied the territory centering on what became the States of New York and Pennsylvania. These Iroquois, sometimes referred to as the "Six Nations" (Seneca, Mohawk, Cayuga, Onondaga, Tuscarora, Oneida) were encountered by the eighteenth-century American white settlers who were moving into this part of the country; and, in the context of the American Revolutionary War, they had a tragic role in the fighting between British and American forces in the years 1777 through 1780. The Seneca War Chief, Chainbreaker (or Tan Wr Nyrs, in his native tongue), played a major part in these events. Years later, as an old man, in 1845-46, in Cold Spring, New York, he tells his story.

It is this narrative that Jeanne Winston Adler relates. She does this in Chainbreaker's own words, as these were recorded at the time; however, this story is amplified throughout its telling by various additions that add greatly to our understanding of the narrative. These include historical and political news accounts of the times; observations from contemporaries of Chainbreaker; and comments from ethnohistorians and anthropologists, including the well-known early scholar, Lewis Henry Morgan, and the ethnologist and archaeologist of more recent times, the late Arthur C. Parker of the New York State Museum at Albany.

The final result is a very readable, fascinating presentation. Although Chainbreaker's account of his life is rooted in the hard evidence of history, it is offered here for the general reader.

Gordon R. Willey
Bowditch Professor Emeritus
Department of Anthropology
Harvard University
April 2001

# Foreword

This book speaks to me personally for two reasons. As a twenty-first-century Seneca, it offers me a window on events more than two centuries ago that had a profound and lasting impact on my people, and what is most rare, it delivers eighteenth-century American history from a Native American perspective—the testimony of the great Seneca war chief and sachem, Chainbreaker. I am also an eighth-generation descendant of Mary Jemison, whose voice acts as counterpoint to Chainbreaker's throughout the following narrative. Over a vast gulf of time and out of the silence of the grave, ancestral voices still speak.

At the start of Chainbreaker's narrative, the Seneca were the largest and most powerful of the Iroquois nations and controlled much of western New York State. The present-day Seneca Nation owns three large tracts of land: the Cattaraugus Reservation, the Allegany Reservation, and the square-mile Oil Springs Reserve near Cuba, New York. I was born in Silver Creek, New York, near the Cattaraugus Reservation, but I grew up in the adjacent town of Irving. Our house stood on Buffalo Road in the "white" part of the town just across the Cattaraugus Creek from the Reservation. An old car bridge spanned the creek near our house, and as a young boy I used to run across it almost daily to visit my cousins and grandmother who lived on the Reservation. My parents belonged to the Episcopal church and our family's social life centered around church activities—lunches, dinners, and picnics—during my childhood. You either belonged to the church or to the Longhouse community then, but my mother and father took me to the Longhouse sometimes at mid-winter, usually to the one at Tonawanda.

The beauty of the Indian world attracted me always. At Christmas, the Thomas Indian School—a boarding school that is closed now—held a bazaar with craftspeople and Indian foods. The art and colors and the delicious smells dazzled me. The rich shades of the blankets warmed you to look at them; the scent of cornbread and corn soup filled the air.

Seneca children made up about forty-five percent of the student body at the Irving Union School for grades one through eight. When I was a very small child, a cruel incident occurred there that made a strong impression on me. A little girl from the Reservation came to school with a dirty dress and uncombed hair. Perhaps her face was dirty, too. The teacher criticized her for it and humiliated her, and I thought, "You don't like her—she's Indian—and you don't like me either because *I'm* Indian."

In my sixth-grade year, the Town of Silver Creek built a centralized school where I attended junior high school and high school. Seneca students formed only about fifteen percent of the whole at Silver Creek, yet I was happy there, an outgoing boy with friends in all groups, who received special praise in art classes, excelled in track, wrestled, and played football, and served as vice-president of his sophomore class. Today, I sometimes wonder how much my light skin—I am fair-skinned in comparison with my cousins—contributed to my success at Silver Creek.

I grew away from my friends on the Reservation at this time, wanting to fit in with the larger school world during my teenaged years. Still, every summer from the age of fifteen I inhabited a strikingly multi-cultural environment, working alongside Indians, African Americans, and Italian immigrants in a big canning factory in Irving. This factory processed the corn, beans, tomatoes, and beets produced on the farms of the area. Puerto Rican migrants filled Irving every summer to work on the farms and in the orchards of Chautauqua County.

In 1962 I entered Buffalo State University as one of only three Native American freshmen out of a class of more than two hundred. I used to see one fellow, a Mohawk, frequently. There was a bond there, but we never said much about our backgrounds. I dated a girl whose mother was a Seneca, and she never referred to her ancestry at all. I only discovered the fact years later. That was the mindset then; many people didn't assert their native identities or cultures, even with other Native Americans. But, in some way, despite these pressures, my core identity remained Seneca.

I traveled in the South twice during my college years, once to Florida on spring break and once on the way to work in the Bahamas. It was a shock to my nineteen and twenty-year-old sensibility to see all the "White Only" signs above restaurants and restrooms, and I never set foot in one of those places. I ate in the "Colored" restaurants and got some pretty strange looks, though no one ever challenged me directly.

After graduation, with my fine arts degree in hand, I went to New York City to work selling art supplies and creating window displays for the Design Research Stores while trying to break into the city's art world. I enjoyed some startling early success with an abstract painting shown at the Tibor de Nagy Gallery on 57th Street in 1968, but even that did not prevent my plunge into a months-long depression. I felt a sense of futility and emptiness as a young Native American man trying to swim alone in a vast, cosmopolitan city.

I returned to Buffalo to teach at Lafayette High School, and then headed west to California. This was a time of political reawakening among many Native Americans. In 1970, members of various Indian nations occupied Alcatraz Island to demand its return to Indian hands. This event had a big impact on me and caused me to truly examine my Indian identity for the first time. Abandoning the abstract images that had absorbed me since college, I began to return to painting the natural world. I showed some of this new work at the Museum of the American Indian at 155th Street in Manhattan (since 1980 renamed the National Museum of the American Indian and relocated to Washington, DC). The Soho Gallery of American Art gave me a one-person show in 1972, and at age twenty-seven, I saw this new work appear on the *Today Show* and in *Art in America* magazine.

With a small grant, I then created a traveling exhibit of works of Iroquois artists, some of whom I had met through the Museum of the American Indian. I also visited each Iroquois community to recruit more artists, and then revisited the communities with the exhibit. I drove to reservations all over New York State. I hung the art works, sometimes arranged activities to accompany the show, answered questions, spoke to the chiefs. With each show, I seemed to take another step deeper into the Iroquois domain and into my Seneca heritage.

The traveling exhibit led to a position as director of the Seneca Nation Education Program, which oversaw the placement of teachers' aides in communities to provide remedial education. I expanded the program by hiring elders to teach traditional Seneca crafts and the Seneca language. Within a short time, Carson Waterman, another Seneca artist, and I founded the Seneca Nation Organization for the Visual Arts (SNOVA), headquartered at Cattaraugus Reservation first. We also had teachers on the Allegany Reservation; later, I was living there and administering our grant. Our mission was to rescue, encourage, and revive a wealth of traditional Seneca arts and crafts practiced by a wide range of craftspeople: basket makers, woodcarvers, stone carvers, silversmiths, and those employing cornhusks, feathers, beads, leather, bark, and many other natural materials.

Contact with craftspeople and native artists enriched my own art immeasurably.

I also supported myself for a while as an ironworker. My father was a union ironworker, and he had obtained employment for me during some of my undergraduate summers. In the 1960s I had worked as a union ironworker doing the rigging in big buildings under construction in Buffalo. Rigging involves moving heavy equipment in and out of buildings using cranes and cribs built from hardwood planking on hardwood rollers. It's brutally hard, dangerous work. Many Iroquois are ironworkers, not just the St. Regis Mohawks, who have acquired a special fame in the field. Is it something within our culture that urges us toward this extreme work to prove that we are the bravest, strongest, toughest? As a non-union ironworker in 1976-77, I worked outside all winter, even during the blizzard of 1977 when the temperature was fifteen degrees below zero with a wind chill of thirty-five below. Union men went after us as well, once cornering our group in a bar; the assailants had pool cues and guns in their cars and I learned what it was to be afraid for your life, and to fight for your life, too.

In 1978, I headed back to New York City to run the newly-formed American Indian Community House Gallery where I curated exhibitions drawing on a nationwide network of Native American artists. Then, in 1985 I came home to western New York to serve as site manager of Ganondagan, the New York State Historic Site in Victor, New York, where the famed

Seneca hilltown once flourished. In 1687, a French army burned Ganondagan and its palisaded granary as part of an effort to destroy the Seneca, their competitors in the international fur trade. The Seneca Nation survived the French assault and became one of the mightiest of the Six Nations during the eighteenth century. Seneca continued to revere the Ganondagan hill site and nearby burial grounds on Boughton Hill. They referred to Ganondagan as "The Town of Peace," and honored the memory and burial place of a Ganondagan woman known as "Mother of Nations" who had assisted the "Peacemaker" at the time of the founding of the Haudenosaunee Confederacy or Iroquois League. Ganondagan also lies only twenty miles from Canandaigua Lake where, according to legend, the first Seneca emerged from the earth of South Hill on the borders of the lake.

Over the last seventeen years, I have worked with consultants to revive the pre- and post-battle history of Ganondagan and also to revive the physical site itself, which appeared to be little more than an abandoned farm in 1985. Thus, I was pleased to read Jeanne Winston Adler's "revival" and "reconstruction" of Chainbreaker's great saga. While Chainbreaker does not speak of Ganondagan in his narrative, it is very likely that he visited this location of such great fame in the Seneca world. He certainly passed near it on several journeys recounted in the narrative. It pleases me to think of Chainbreaker here. While his narrative is mostly an account of Revolutionary War actions and battles, there are glimpses of his deeper spiritual beliefs, his comfort and oneness with the elements of nature, and his strong love of family and community. Activities at present-day Ganondagan, with its authentic, full-size, Seneca bark longhouse, visitor center, and nature trails, also celebrate these traditional values.

> G. Peter Jemison
> Ganondagan
> November, 2001

# Chainbreaker Speaks

In the winter of 1845–46, an old man sits by his fireside in Cold Spring, New York, and tells a remarkable story. He speaks of the time he was a young warrior of the Seneca Nation and fought for "the King across the Great Waters" in battles of the American Revolution.

The eighty-seven-year-old[1] sachem or high chief is still a man of surprising vigor. (Four years into the future, a visitor will claim that the sachem appears no older than an average man in his middle sixties.) He measures a full six feet in height and possesses ample, flowing, grey-white hair. His intelligent, heavy-lidded eyes gaze out from slightly hollowed eye sockets; these, and a strong, aquiline nose, give his face a hawk-like appearance. The European-descended Americans, who flourish all around him, call the old sachem Blacksnake, or Governor Blacksnake, but the people of his own Seneca world know him as Tan Wr Nyrs, or Chainbreaker.

The old man speaks in the Seneca language to a fellow Seneca, Hah Na I Sah, or Benjamin Williams, though certain fragments of his tale are probably conveyed in English. (Consider the authentic British cadence of the words that Chainbreaker puts into the mouth of a "British commissioner": "Very good, Sir. Thank you all.

---

[1] His age, according to his own narrative.

19

We will firstly go to dinner and drink rum and sugar.")
Chainbreaker claims not to speak or understand any
English. Does he reject the tongue out of pride? An early
settler of the Susquehanna region of New York once said
of a "fine-looking" Delaware woman: "She would not
allow herself to speak English. She did so however, once;
there was a man drowning and she informed a white man
on the bank where he had sunk."[1]

Hah Na I Sah, the translator, is a tall, thin, rather pale-
skinned man of middle age. He is a Christian and deplores
Chainbreaker's loyalty to Iroquois religious beliefs.
Despite this conflict, the younger man, like Chainbreaker,
springs from one of the aristocratic Seneca families and is
old enough to remember much of traditional Seneca society. In many ways, he is the perfect interviewer for the
aged sachem.

We can imagine the two men sitting together before
Chainbreaker's hearth: Hah Na I Sah's dark head bent
over a sheaf of papers; the sachem's near-white head held
erect as he looks into the distance at faraway events. The
two are not alone. Dark-eyed children play between bark
boxes and cornhusk baskets ranged along the log walls of
the dwelling. Every so often, a young woman, one of
Chainbreaker's great-granddaughters, comes forward to
stir corn soup simmering over the fire. There are other
adults present, too, on this cold winter's day—a handful
of middle-aged or elderly men and women settled upon a
long bench. Chainbreaker has a large family, and many

[1] Statement of Jesse McQuigg, "Draper Manuscripts," Wisconsin Historical
Society, Series 17F, p. 63.

members live nearby or under this roof. Unlike his friend Red Jacket, who saw all five of his children die before him, Chainbreaker has been more fortunate. Fourteen years later, Hah Na I Sah will write a letter that reveals Chainbreaker's constant care for his family: ". . . he [Chainbreaker] then believed himself that he is not going to live many Days more, although he was not ill, thought he was a weak and low speech But no sickness the Next Day eat hardy at dinner and called to his grand children to his bed side and give them good advice, and Remember his advices and to love their father and mother and love to each other &c, as soon as he got through talking, he then went act so he was a Sleep about 15 minute he was then Died . . ."[1]

But today Chainbreaker is still strong. He sits at his ease in a long blue shirt of machine-spun and -woven cotton and a pair of trousers of brown home-spun and -woven wool. The hands of white women—and some men—have prepared every fiber that clothes him. But, elk-hide moccasins, well tanned, rubbed and stitched by Seneca hands, cradle and warm his feet. Chainbreaker utters the liquid, slightly bubbling, Iroquoian words, and all the faces—soft, young, butter-colored faces, and old, weathered, mahogany ones—turn towards him. Let us gather round the sachem, too, and hear his story.

---

[1] Letter of Benjamin Williams/Hah Na I Sah, dated January 14, 1860, "Draper Manuscripts," Wisconsin Historical Society, Series 16F, p. 247.

# Editor's Note

In this new rendering of Chainbreaker's narrative, standard English spelling, punctuation, grammar, and syntax "correct" Hah Na I Sah's prose. (The excerpt from Hah Na I Sah's letter on Chainbreaker's death is one example of his unaltered prose.) Here, modern words occasionally replace archaic ones. "I was very engaged to know" becomes "I was very eager to know," for instance. But most archaic words remain in the text, followed by bracketed explanations. At two specific points only—the section of Chapter Four dealing with Chainbreaker's parents' lives and the section of Chapter Eight on the councils following Fort Stanwix—the order of some sentences or paragraphs shifts to present the narrator's account more clearly.

For improved readability, many "then"s, "next"s, and "so"s also disappear from this text, along with a few repetitive sentences. The goal was always to present Chainbreaker's statement in lucid, grammatical form. After all, he spoke Seneca grammatically. Therefore, phrases such as "the canoes got built" are re-phrased here.

Names of individuals appear in a uniform way throughout the edited narrative. Cornplanter is always Cornplanter and never John O'Bail, his "white" name; Chainbreaker is never Blacksnake. Likewise, the "British commissioner" always steps forth named by this explicit two-word phrase in the edited version, though he is often simply the "commissioner" in Hah Na I Sah's text. The place name of the Seneca town, Canawagus, also replaces Hah Na I Sah's use of "Avon," the name of the white town built near Canawagus' ruins. In the same way, the "Fort George" of the original narrative becomes "Fort Niagara"; the British built Fort George, on the west bank of the Niagara River, only after they ceded east-bank Fort Niagara to the Americans in 1796.

The new narrative takes its greatest departure from the original manuscript in the matter of certain pronouns. The first two paragraphs of Chapter One were set down by Hah Na I Sah in the third person ("he" rather than "I"), and much of Captain Hudson's story in Chapter Six appears in Hah Na I Sah's version as a tale told in the third person plural ("they") with only a single paragraph in the first person plural ("we"). But those few "we"s indicated, to this editor's mind, that Chainbreaker was present during the episode, and so pronouns change to agree with this idea.

Another departure involves the rationalization of all year dates cited by Hah Na I Sah. According to his original transcription, many of the events of the Revolutionary War took place in the 1760s! In the revised narrative, Chainbreaker's birth date agrees with his stated age of "sixteen" at the time of the summons to the Pittsburgh Council in 1775. It must be pointed out that in his 1850 interview with the historian Lyman Draper, Chainbreaker claimed a greater age. He told Draper that he had been twenty-two years old in 1775—not sixteen. Actually, he simply told Draper that, according to his parents, he (Chainbreaker) was two years old "when Sir William Johnson defeated the French at Lake George [1755]"[1] and then Draper did the arithmetic. How accurate was the parents' recollection? One can't help noting that Johnson and the British forces enjoyed their greatest and final victory over the French at Montreal in late 1760. If Chainbreaker had been born in January 1759—he thought he had a winter birth time—he would have been close to two years old when this last victory occurred.

Though a greater age accords better with Chainbreaker's leadership role from 1777 or 1778 onwards, the narrative contains a number of internal clues that seem to support the younger age. Would a twenty-two-year-old warrior rate as "nothing but a passenger" in the party attending the 1776 council at German Flats? Likewise, is Chainbreaker truly an almost middle-aged thirty-nine when he falls in love with the "Osage" maiden out west, and Captain Hudson's disapproval causes him such "sorrow"? And Chainbreaker stresses his own youth at the 1792 meeting with Washington. Washington must take him by the hand and draw Chainbreaker into the gun shop since the young chief "did not want to put [himself] too far forward." Thus, this rendering of the sachem's account accepts and does not "correct" the ages recorded by Hah Na I Sah.

The necessary editing changes free Chainbreaker's voice at last. And what a story he tells—though we must remember, it is a story told by an aged man attempting to

[1] Lyman Draper, "Draper Manuscripts," Wisconsin Historical Society, Series S, No. 4, p. 1.

recall and order a whirlwind of violent events. Scholars know that some of his facts are wrong. Curiously, he told both Hah Na I Sah and a later interviewer, the adopted Seneca, Peter Crouse, that he had acquired the name Chainbreaker or Tan Wr Nyrs at Oswego in 1777.[1] In fact, Cornplanter held the Tan Wr Nyrs title, an important war leader's position, all through the Revolutionary War. Has the narrator forgotten this? Or is he consciously inflating his wartime role?

In 1850, Chainbreaker presented a different, more accurate, picture to Lyman Draper. According to Draper's notes, at Oswego after Brant and Cornplanter had been acclaimed supreme leaders, " . . . the leading chiefs named to the British a number of active young warriors of their respective tribes, suitable to be appointed war chiefs. These the British leaders accordingly appointed to serve during the war as war-captains or warchiefs . . . Of the Senecas thus appointed, the following are recollected: Cornplanter, Red Jacket, Blacksnake [Chainbreaker], Lake], She-gwoin-de-gue or Little Beard, Hi-a-de-o-ni, Hah-no-gwus or He-Who-Skims-the Floating-Grease, Hah-sque-sah-ah, Dah-wah-dee-ho, Gah-nah-a-ge, Dah-gai-ond, Da-oh-joc-doh, and others."[2] So the young Chainbreaker served as just one of a number of war chiefs. A brave, athletic, young man, nephew of a sachem, might well have led a war band at eighteen, though some

[1] Letter of Peter Crouse to Lyman Draper, July 27, 1850, "Draper Manuscripts," Wisconsin Historical Society, Series F, no. 16.
[2] Lyman Draper, "Conversations with Governor Blacksnake," Feb. 10-20, 1850, in "Draper Manuscripts," Wisconsin Historical Society, Series S, No. 4, p. 20.

critical readers may suspect that the narrator really became a war captain in 1778—after he had proved himself at the Battle of Oriskany.

Chainbreaker evidently went by the name Dahgr Yan Doh, or by some other now-unknown name, during the course of most of the events he describes—which calls into question the use of the Chainbreaker name throughout the following account. But then, Cornplanter, also, did not acquire his famous name until after the Revolution. A completely rational revision of Hah Na I Sah's manuscript is not possible. While "Canawagus" substitutes for the anachronistic "Avon" here, Hah Na I Sah's word "Indians" stands, though certainly an odd term for the narrator to employ. "Cayuga Lake" also remains as Chainbreaker's stated birthplace, though Draper's 1850 interview notes contradict this fact, instead citing Seneca Lake as the sachem's true birthplace. Had Hah Na I Sah mixed up the English names for the two lakes? It is possible the translator made the same kind of English language mistake by calling Shawnee "Osages;" however, this rendering leaves Hah Na I Sah's "Osages" in place.

Some of the battles that Chainbreaker describes cannot be firmly matched up with known battles. Are the events retold at the beginning of Chapter Five really an account of the November 1778 attack on Cherry Valley, New York, rather than the July 1778 attack on the Wyoming Valley in Pennsylvania? This editor favors the second view and places the statements of survivors of the "Wyoming Massacre" adjacent to Chainbreaker's story here. But there are problems with this identification, as there are with the identification of the battle named here as Wyalusing.

Without doubt, the actions of various battles became intertwined and mixed in the mind of the old sachem. But this doesn't detract from the psychological truth of his account. The narrative presents his authentic, internal experience of the war: the fear, confusion, and exultation of the engagements; his pride in the noble and generous deeds of fellow Seneca like Captain Hudson; his dislike of the Mohawk Joseph Brant; and many other things as well.

By the end of his story, we know him well. The Chainbreaker of the narrative is an outgoing optimist who prefers not to think of negative things. He enjoys remembering his own bravery, skill, luck, endurance, and generosity, and that of his friends. It gives him pleasure to think of the honorable, and mostly honored part, Cornplanter and Red Jacket played at the councils with the British and Americans, of successful hunts and fine dances, and of one particular girl briefly encountered many years before. Yet, painful things loom all around the edges of his story and often come into the heart of it. Thus, there is great poignancy to his brave recital.

Chainbreaker tells us about the carnage of a number of battlefields, but (probably) nothing about Cherry Valley, where he was present and where, unlike their actions at Wyoming, the Iroquois did kill women and children in their homes. And when the war comes home to the Iroquois in 1779, he shows us Red Eyes and his people and the Onondaga as victims, but says nothing about the fate of his hometown, Canawagus, which was probably burned, and nothing of the starvation faced by his own townspeople. Chainbreaker's stiff upper lip means that the voice of another Seneca, Mary Jemison, often accompanies his account. She does speak of negative things: the grief after the losses at Oriskany (brushed off by Chainbreaker) and the hunger of 1779–1780. Therefore, Mary Jemison and others, some contemporaries of Chainbreaker and some not, break into the narrative from time to time with added information and experiences. These excerpts have been drawn from a variety of sources, published and unpublished, outlined in detail in the bibliography at the close of the book.

What is the value of Chainbreaker's narrative? It is his voice, above all, which survives through and despite the workings of two editor/translators. In some ways, Chainbreaker's account resembles a Homeric epic of the Revolutionary War time. It's not an epic crafted in verse, but it contains passages of wonderful language: "I saw many narrow places, and close to hand"; "we ran against them and went amongst them with force and slew them with tomahawk and swords, and destroyed them all"; "death is the death." Even non-poetic sections of the narrative exert a curious power and charm. Perhaps they contain an indefinable kind of poetry. Through Chainbreaker's story, we also step into an exotic place: the mind and memory of an eighteenth-century warrior.

## CHAPTER ONE

# "No People Can Live More Happy"

*From the earliest beginnings of their distinctive culture, the Iroquois peoples lived in the broad, rich-loamed river valleys of central New York and Pennsylvania. Sometime before European settlers began to arrive on the eastern shores of North America, perhaps one hundred and fifty years before, two leaders, Deganawida and Hiawatha, united five Iroquois nations—the Seneca, the Cayuga, the Onondaga, the Oneida, and the Mohawk—into the Great Peace of the Iroquois League. These five peoples not only swore to keep the peace with one another, but also extended this peace to other, tributary nations.*

*The Iroquois compared their league to one of their own bark-covered dwellings, called longhouses, which held many fires and many families within a single structure. The Seneca, who lived about Seneca Lake and westward on the Genesee*

River (and later on the Allegheny River), were called the "Keepers of the Western Door" of this symbolic longhouse. The territories of the Cayuga, Onondaga, Oneida, and Mohawk stretched eastward, in that order. The Mohawk territory—the Mohawk Valley and portions of the Hudson River Valley—served as the "Eastern Door." The Onondaga in the center were the "Firekeepers" who maintained the sacred council fire where delegates of all the nations met to deliberate. In 1712, after English settlers drove the Iroquoian-speaking Tuscarora out of South Carolina, this group joined the confederacy too. The Five Nations gave the Tuscarora lands adjoining the Oneida and Onondaga. In this way, the Five Nations became the Six Nations.

Cross-national clans helped to bind the Iroquois League together. The different nations each boasted from three to eight or nine clans named for animal spirits or totems. Wolf, Turtle, and Bear were, and still are, the most common Iroquois clans. Others are Hawk, Heron, Snipe, Deer, and Beaver. Each Iroquois child is born into the clan of his or her mother and then, traditionally, marries outside that clan. But even in the eighteenth century, some people broke the marriage rule; both of Chainbreaker's parents belonged to the Wolf Clan.

On the eve of the American Revolution, the Seneca were the most numerous and most powerful of all the Iroquois nations. They controlled all the lands from Seneca Lake to Lake Erie. Alongside lush fields of corn, beans, and squash, they tended gardens filled with carrots, peas, cucumbers, and watermelons. They also raised cattle and pigs and maintained large peach and apple orchards. Many had replaced their old pole and bark-shingle houses with sturdy, axe-cut log houses containing brick chimneys and occasionally even glass-paned *windows. A number of the Seneca towns, including Chainbreaker's Canawagus, held one thousand to two thousand inhabitants.*

*Eight lords, or sachems, ruled over the Seneca Nation, always chosen by the women of certain privileged families. Sub-rulers, or chiefs, played a role in the nation's government, also. Throughout the eighteenth century, the Seneca possessed around twice as many chiefs as sachems—about twenty. Many of the chiefs won their positions on the basis of merit alone, like Chainbreaker's friend, the great orator, Red Jacket (c. 1750-1830).*

*The semi-hereditary sachemships tended to pass from uncle to nephew. Thus, Chainbreaker eventually succeeded his uncle, Cornplanter. Cornplanter and Chainbreaker shared another office in sequence, also: a war leader's position, known as the Tan Wr Nyrs. This title, limited to men of the Wolf Clan, was a very important one. Along with another Senecan war leader, the So No So Wa, chosen from the Turtle Clan, the Tan Wr Nyrs traditionally led all Six Nations' forces in any league-wide war.*

*Why did Seneca fill the two top generalships of the League? This situation probably arose from the Seneca Nation's post at the "Western Door," facing many hostile peoples. Seneca warriors were famous for their fighting skills, their large stature, and their bravery.*

My real name, Tan Wr Nyrs, means chain-breaker. This name was given to me at the time I became Chief Warrior at the commencement of the Indian Wars of the American Revolution. But during my boyhood I was called Dahgr Yan Doh, until I became a young man, then Tan Wr Nyrs or Chainbreaker, following the custom of changing names on reaching manhood. If you gamble all at once at one place or bet something all at once, you will say Dahgr Yan Doh. That is the meaning of my first name.

I was a chief commander in the wars together with Cornplanter, Red Jacket and Brant. We, the most principal men, performed hard labor during the American Revolution, till peace was declared. After this, Washington and the Six Nations of Indians made treaties and peace. I then became Grand Sachem of the Seneca Nation.

I was born near Cayuga Lake in the year 1759 and immediately moved from there to the Village of Canawagus on the Genesee River, in consequence of having connections

"Gusga-e-sa-ta, or Deer Buttons [an Iroquois gambling game] . . . Eight buttons, about an inch in diameter, were made of elk-horn, and having been rounded and polished, were slightly burned upon one side to blacken them . . . Two persons spread a blanket and seated themselves upon it. One of them shook the deer-buttons in his hands, and then threw them down. If six turned up of the same color, it counted two, if seven, it counted four, and if all, it counted twenty . . ."

*Lewis Henry Morgan, 1818-1881, ethnologist and adopted member of the Seneca Nation*

there on my father's side and on my mother's side who were all desirous that my father and mother and all the family should move to Canawagus. So they did—in the year 1761. Here I was raised and brought up to be a young man. The people much liked me, especially my companions, but I was agreeable with all men and kind, and the people placed confidence and trust in me.

Deer buttons

When I was about sixteen years of age, I began to hear that something was wrong between Great Britain and America—a great deal of disturbances between them—for what reason I did not know. In fact, I did not pretend to know much of any such things, until my uncle, Cornplanter, was called along with others by the Americans; notice was sent out from Albany to hold a council or convention at Pittsburgh. I then supposed it must be something concerning these disturbances, and I began to take notice of our chiefs' councils' affairs.

In the month of April 1775, the messenger from Albany arrived at Canawagus. Red Jacket and Cornplanter were then the head men among the Seneca chiefs and the

"When I was a child I played with the butterfly, the grasshopper, and the frog . . ."
*Cornplanter, 1743–1836, Seneca warchief and sachem*

"My grandmother used to make me go into the water every morning, the first thing I did as soon as I got up in the summertime. I got up from my bed with my robe round my body and went to the water before I was dressed . . . in wintertime, grandmother used to throw one pailful of cold water on me before I got up in the morning. I always supposed this to be a benefit to me—to make me tough and smart and of strong constitution. She always taught me so, and I believed what she told me and was often going into the river when it was cold and freezing. She also wanted me to learn to be a good swimmer, and so, many times, I went into the river and swam across with some load on my back, across and back again."
*Captain John Decker, 1746–1851, Seneca war chief*

other nations of Indians connected with the Iroquois. They had considerable influence amongst all the other tribes, and they concluded it would be necessary to attend the Pittsburgh Convention, according to invitation. All the Longhouse met at Canawagus, and the different nations consented to appoint their own delegations of chiefs and warriors. I was particularly invited to go along with them.

So we went to work to make preparations to start and to provide who was to stay at home. When all was ready, several chiefs and warriors started from Canawagus. We struck a westerly course and came into Lake Erie about eight miles above the mouth of Buffalo Creek. We traveled on the lake shore and went on up as far as Erie Village in Pennsylvania. There were then but a few houses in this village, one or two provision stores and a tavern. Thence from this place, we headed south and came into a

Longhouse of the Seneca-Iroquois

A real, physical long-house:

"The long house was generally from fifty to a hundred and thirty feet in length, by about sixteen in width, with partitions at intervals of about ten or twelve feet, or two lengths of the body. Each apartment was, in fact, a separate house, having a fire in the centre, and accommodating two families, one upon each side of the fire. Thus a house one hundred and twenty feet long would contain ten fires and twenty families . . . it was sided up, and shingled with red elm or ash bark, the rough side out. The bark was flattened and dried, and then cut in the form of boards . . . At the two ends of the house were doors, either of bark hung upon hinges of wood, or of deer or bear-skins suspended before the opening; and however long the house, or whatever the number of fires, these were the only entrances."

*Lewis Henry Morgan*

stream above what is now called Midville, and thence on down French Creek, which empties into the Allegheny River.

We had several days' travel before we came out to the mouth of French Creek, where there were three or four log cabins of white people, first settlers. There we made a stop and camped out in this neighborhood for several days in order to build bark canoes to go down the river as far as Pittsburgh. While we stayed in this white neighborhood, the oldest man used to visit us and bring bread timber [*breadstuff*] for us to eat, and we used to give him every time fresh venison. Sometimes we took five or six deer every day while we stayed at this place, until we had built sufficient bark canoes to carry our number downstream.

We canoed downstream on the Allegheny River. This was already about the fall of the year 1775, so we made a stop seven miles from Franklin over the winter, at a place now called Big Sandy Creek. On the first day of January 1776, we arrived at Pittsburgh from Big Sandy. Several white men came to see us on the same afternoon. The news went to the commissioner's ears that we were come, and he visited us. He introduced himself to us and to Cornplanter and Red Jacket and to the several other chiefs of the several different nations of Indians, all proper delegates, and we conversed with him. He appointed a certain ground on which to meet the next morning and set several men to work to make seats in the open field.

In the morning, Uncle Cornplanter advised our company to hold one mind and name Red Jacket for speaker in the meeting. We made all prepared on our part and went onto the ground.

The commissioner said, "We, the white people, have long desired to make known to you, brothers, the difficulties existing between America and the King of Great Britain. Great Britain's government uses us badly, and the American people endeavor to have freedom to build up our own government. The King has ordered his armies and warriors to fight us. We therefore ask our red brethren, the Six Nations and others, not to join either party.

"We will lay down our lives for our independence and freedom, and we feel an interest in and are desirous of your welfare as independent nations. Don't lift up your hands against America or Great Britain. We and they, alone, got into difficulty. We wish you to stand neutral and be at peace with all your white brethren, and if we should lose our liberty, then we will be under Great Britain's government. We are poor; the King is rich. But God looks upon us. If we are right, he will help us to gain our liberty,

"... as the canoe birch did not grow within the home territories of the Iroquois, they generally used the red-elm, and bitter-nut-hickory ... Having taken off a bark of the requisite length and width, and removed the rough outside, it was shaped in the canoe form. Rim pieces of white-ash, or other elastic wood, of the width of the hand, were then run around the edge, outside and in, and stitched through and through with the bark itself. In stitching, they used bark thread or twine, and splints. The ribs consisted of narrow strips of ash, which were set about a foot apart along the bottom of the canoe, and having been turned up the sides, were secured under the rim ... In size, these canoes varied from twelve feet with sufficient capacity to carry two men, to forty feet with sufficient capacity for thirty."
*Lewis Henry Morgan*

"After the conclusion of the French War [1763] our tribe had nothing to trouble it till the commencement of the Revolution. For twelve or fifteen years the use of the implements of war was not known, nor the war-whoop heard, save on days of festivity . . ."

*Mary Jemison, 1742–1833, captive—later adopted member—of the Seneca Nation*

and we are to look to him for our favors."

Red Jacket gave the answer: "Brothers, we are Indians and citizens of this island. God made us to inhabit here and grow large in number, and he gives us all we need to enjoy. We have a large number of our red brethren and never yet had wars or difficulties worthwhile to mention.

"Our Maker protects us through our lives and provides for us. All colors of his children are under the heavens. We give thanks to God, who gathers us together this day and gives us clean ears to hear you speaking to us. We understand you and acknowledge your words are important to hear. We will take your words and advice with us to our people and lay the subject before them. We are not authorized or empowered to complete this object [*purpose*], therefore we will leave it to our people. The business will be done by a majority, and we will send you a delegation to carry the answer of our people."

The commissioner replied, "Brothers and friends, open a good ear. This is a family quarrel between us and Old England. You Indians are not concerned in it. We don't wish you to take up the hatchet against the King's troops. We desire you to remain at home and not join either side, but keep the hatchet buried deep. We ask you to love peace and maintain it, that the path may be kept open with all our people and yours, to pass and re-pass without molestation. Brothers, we live on the same ground with you; the same island is our common birthplace. We desire to sit down under the same tree of peace with you.

"This is all I have to say, and I feel satisfied with what you have said in answer. And I wish you this afternoon to take a walk with me and visit a new garrison."

So we all went with him. There were only a few regular warriors in garrison and a few pieces of cannon and balls for them. The United States' [*actually Continental Congress'*] commissioner ordered us to go to the provision store to get what we wanted while we stayed in that place. Near night, we returned to our camp at the mouth of Monongahela, and

"I am Dekanawideh and with the Five Nations' confederate lords I plant the Tree of the Great Peace. I plant it in your territory Adodarhoh and the Onondaga Nation, in the territory of you who are fire keepers.

"I name the tree the Tree of the Great Long Leaves. Under the shade of this Tree of the Great Peace we spread the soft, white, feathery down of the globe thistle as seats for you, Adodarhoh and your cousin lords . . . If any man of any nation outside of the Five Nations shall show a desire to obey the laws of the Great Peace . . . they shall be welcomed to take shelter beneath the Tree of the Long Leaves."

*Account of the founding of the Iroquois Confederacy in* **The Constitution of the Five Nations**

the next morning we made preparations to start for home. Some of our bark canoes we cast away; three canoes we kept to carry our provision in as we came up the river. Some of us came on foot, and some pushing our canoes upstream. We came on, about ten miles that day, and we kept going every day and came back the same way we had gone, and we reached home, Canawagus on the Genesee River, in the month of June 1776.

As soon as we had rested, we called a council at Canawagus and gave invitation to all the Indian nations, not only to the Six Nations, but to all who had an interest in the subject. Notice was given to braves and messengers who traveled to the east and south and west and north.

So we held a council fire to spit out what we had heard at Pittsburgh. Joseph Brant [*1742–1807, Mohawk chief and brother-in-law of British Indian agent, Sir William Johnson*] was present this time. Red Jacket stood and told all the words over again that we had heard from the commissioner at Pittsburgh. Joseph Brant made considerable controversy for a while amongst the people. He felt prejudiced against us for desiring to take the advice of the commissioner who made the council fire at Pittsburgh. But Brant did not succeed in his arguments, and he agreed with us after a while and reconciled with us. But the council lacked one nation of Indians—the Delaware from Susquehanna—and therefore was postponed for sixty days.

In the meantime, a messenger from the East arrived, bringing notice of another great council to be held at Albany, called by Washington's commissioner. This was in the month of August 1776. So our chiefs consulted on the subject, and they concluded they would pay attention. Again, they gave out and sent out messengers to every adjacent settlement of the different tribes of Indians. I was one of the messengers sent to the tribes twenty miles east of Canawagus to give them ten days' notice to convene at the Canawagus longhouse.

The chiefs of every nation met and considered whether some warriors would be needed to go with the chiefs to the Albany council fire. The question was thrown to the warriors to pass their own opinions. We consulted together alone and concluded that whoever wished to go, he might go. Also, a place was named where we would all meet together on the way, and a day set to start from home.

All the Senecas from Canawagus went, chiefs and warriors, and reached the appointed meeting place the evening of the first day's travel. During the night, we talked on the subject for which we were going to the open council fire, concerning the quarrels of the father and his son. We considered it important to see clearly, with the naked eyes, and to open our ears to hear truth and to see where we were going. In this company, the majority wanted "to be somebody" and to walk with heads up and see what was going on. They did not want to hold their heads over and see nothing. This was the consultation of the Six Nations during that night.

The next morning, every man took baggage and went on the trail towards Albany. We traveled this day together and stayed together on the second

"Yesterday some of the Cayugas arrived and the Remainder are expected to Day. The Senecas, it is said, will be here to Morrow, if so, the Conference will begin on the next Day. I sincerely wish it was ended. The Consumption of provision and Rum is incredible. It equals that of an army of three thousand Men; altho' the Indians here are not above twelve hundred, including Men, Women and Children."
*Philip Schuyler, General of the Continental Army, in a letter dated August 2, 1776*

night; the next day we divided companies. On the fifth
day's travel, we arrived at Albany.

There was a large number already assembled with
white people and officers. The officers told us that the
assembly had been expecting us on the place every hour
and was waiting for us to forward the business. One officer told the chiefs to go to a certain office to get orders on
some provision stores for each nation of Indians who came
with the companies. Cornplanter himself, and all the rest
went to get the orders. Uncle Cornplanter gave me the
order for the Senecas' provisions, and several others went
with me, and all the rest went after their nations' shares.

So we obtained provisions enough that night, and we
all went to the edge of the woods to build our tents so we
could be by ourselves. All the other tribes did the same.
There, we laid down by the fireside, comfortable that night,
and slept well—I supposing the next morning I should hear
something new to me. And I felt very eager to hear whatever would be laid before us and to consider it.

The next morning after breakfast, the white people
began to gather at the ground of the council fire, and soon
after, one of the officers came to us and called upon us to

Tomahawk

come onto the ground. He took us far onto it, where it had been reserved for us to sit. Immediately after we sat down, Washington's commissioner appeared in the midst of the congregation. He moved his face towards us and said:

"We are the white people. We are descendants from old countries across the big waters, and you are the citizens of this country. You are the Indians of different nations, of great numbers of each nation, and we therefore call upon you, to consult with us as a deed of friendship. Last spring your Six Nations permitted you to meet with us at Pittsburgh to hear of the difficulties in the King's family. It is our own business. We, the Americans, have determined to depart from Great Britain's government, and we have made our own rules and laws and have united with several states of this America. We will stand against the British in the hour of need—either to conquer or to fall for our liberty.

"You have nothing to do with our father's children's quarrels, and we therefore wish you to live in peace. We also desire to get along without putting you to any trouble. As we have said to you before, keep your tomahawk and knives

"The tomahawk succeeded the war-club, as the rifle did the bow. . . . They are made of steel, brass, or iron. The choicer articles are surmounted by a pipe-bowl, and have a perforated handle, that they may answer the double purpose of ornament and use. In such the handle, and often the blade itself, are richly inlaid with silver. It is worn in the girdle, and behind the back, except when in actual battle. They used it in close combat with terrible effect, and also threw it with unerring certainty at distant objects, making it revolve in the air in its flight."
*Lewis Henry Morgan*

War club

down underground. Keep yourselves quiet, and your families at home and at large. You should hold yourselves perfectly independent nations, governed by your own rules and laws."

After supper all the Six Nations were together in the evening to consult with one another. At this time, I was nothing but a "passenger" [*a junior member of the party, with little standing or voice*] amongst the warriors. And to hear all the business going on, it seemed to me very important business, indeed, and very important to understand, and I felt great interest in our people's welfare.

The chiefs gathered at one of the largest firesides, and talked about what the commissioner had said to us. Without trouble, they unanimously agreed that they would take up the advice given to us. The warriors were also well satisfied, for the decision was made by the chiefs and warriors together with all good feeling—which

"I do therefore by this Belt in the name of your Father the great King of England, in behalf of all his American Subjects renew and confirm the Covenant Chain subsisting between us, strengthening it, and rubbing off any rust which it may have contracted that it may appear bright to all Nations as a proof of our love and Friendship . . ."

*Sir William Johnson, from his speech to the Six Nations at the Treaty of Fort Stanwix in 1768*

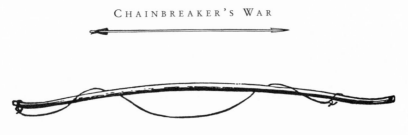

Bow

was considered an important object. So we went to sleep with good feeling for our pillow throughout the night.

In the morning, Red Jacket spoke to the Americans on behalf of the Six Nations: "Brothers, when your fathers crossed the great water and came over to this land, the King of England gave them a talk. He assured them that they and their children would still be his children. If they would leave their native country and make settlements, and buy and sell with their brethren beyond the water, they would still keep hold of the same covenant chain and enjoy peace.

"But where is the covenant chain of peace? It seems that chain has grown rusty, and a puling [*small, weak*], broken one is not good for anything. Where shall you go to have a new one minted and to seek for the forge? You cannot find one, and now you and your men must build one. The King of England interferes with your building of a forge. He says

"The deer ran as plenty as sheep. One might start from the river and go . . . up the creek . . . and see on the way twenty or twenty-five and perhaps as many as that in a drove. We killed them as we wanted them. We could hear the wolves howl in the night. In the winter season when they had driven the deer into the river, they would stand upon the bank and howl. Their lairs were plenty back upon the mountains."

*Jesse McQuigg, b. circa 1770, early settler of Owego, New York*

"... the Turtle dance ... Two Indians spread upon the ground a couple of deer-skins, on which they seated themselves, each holding in the hands a box made of the turtle shell, which enclosed several kernels of corn. They shook these and made them rattle so as to chime with a tune, which they began to sing in a low voice, as a signal for the dance to commence. It was opened by an aged Indian ... and as he advanced into the open space, joined with a low hum in the tune that was singing, and began to dance, making the movements principally on his heels. The next one that came forward was an elderly looking squaw, she had her blanket drawn partly over her head ... Others followed on after them promiscuously, forming themselves into a ring, with their heads most of the time facing the center ..."

*Sketches ... in the Life and Times of Major Moses Van Campen; Van Campen, 1757–1849, was a captive of the Seneca in 1778–1780.*

come to me. But you have determined that you will build one for your own. The King has also determined that you will go to the King. This has created the quarrel.

"It is true that all the Indian nations have nothing to do with your father's children's quarrel. Therefore your opinion is agreeable with ours, and we shall stand neutral and keep hands down for peace."

Washington's commissioner returned thanks to us for the answer we made, and that afternoon, every one of the companions went five miles before retiring for the night. With good feeling towards each other, we there enjoyed ourselves in our united feeling. The next day after breakfast, we started on our way. At noon, we came to a large forest and made a stop for a few days for gathering meat timber by hunting for venison and other provision for our long journey towards home.

I went out to hunt or to see whether there was any game about or nearby this place. After I got out of sight of our fireside, but little away, I saw a number of deer running, coming towards me, and they stopped not far from me. I then had a chance to shoot at one of them, and killed it, and the rest of them did not get out of sight of me. I made haste towards them and made another shot at one and killed that too. I took this deer on my back and carried it to our fireside. I made the rest of the boys go after the other one. The company was very pleased with the two deer for our supper and breakfast.

"No people can live more happy than the Indian did in times of peace. Their lives were a continual round of pleasures. Their wants were few and easily satisfied."
*Mary Jemison*

At this time we had nothing to fear and stayed at this place several days, and then started on again towards Onondaga. There, we made a long visit with the Onondagas. The Onondaga Indians wished us to stay even longer with them, especially those that had been long with us at Albany. But we thought we had stayed long enough, although we had had a great deal of fine times and good dances.

They were so kind to us; I had some notions to stay with them. But my companions would not let me stay, so I had to go home with them to the Genesee River. It was in the fall of the year 1776 when we arrived at our old homestead and found our people in good condition and good health. We remained there peaceably all the winter.

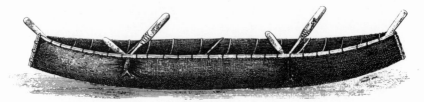

## CHAPTER TWO

# "We Will Go and Attend the Father"

T*he Seneca guarded their neutrality through the spring of 1777, as they had promised at Pittsburgh and at Albany (actually at a place called German Flats, west of Albany). But a three-pronged British campaign was about to sweep them into the Revolutionary War. In the summer of 1777, General Burgoyne led an eight-thousand-man army south, over Lake Champlain and down the Hudson River, heading for Albany. General Howe and another large army proceeded from the Chesapeake to Philadelphia with plans to continue northward to join Burgoyne. Colonel St. Leger with a smaller force drove east from Lake Ontario to Fort Stanwix, which guarded the western end of the Mohawk Valley. Beyond this fort, the Mohawk River Valley formed an open highway leading on to Albany, where all three armies hoped to meet in victory.*

**B**ut in the spring of the year 1777—I was then about eighteen years of my age—a messenger arrived in our country, having the authority of the British government, and notified the chiefs and head men of our Indian nations of a convention on the banks of Lake Ontario on the southeast side of the lake.

The messenger said, "The father wishes to have an arrangement made, for in future time, it may happen our affairs will be disturbed, and he wishes to make all understood in regard to such things."

The sachem [*Cornplanter*] said, "I will give notice to my people and the chiefs also, and we will consider the subject in council with all the Six Nations' brethren. If the Indian chiefs and warriors rest their minds on the subject and favor to go, we will go and attend the Father as he opens and kindles his convention, and will listen and hear what he would say to us."

Within a few days the chiefs and warriors gathered, and a majority favored the question. It was also decided whoever wished to go along, they might go. Young men and young females might also go for witnesses at the meeting with the British. My uncle then invited me to take charge of a certain company to keep them in order.

All the chiefs of the Six Nations and the warriors went, and also our women went along with us. They went mostly for fear that the invitation might be a snare or something dangerous created by the redcoat warriors. But when we arrived there at the place appointed, at the

Male legging

ground for the council fire or convention, immediately the officers came to us, to see what was wanted and to supply us with provisions and with the flood of rum. Some amongst our warriors made use of this intoxicating drink. There were several barrels delivered to us for us to drink. The white man told us to drink as much as we wanted of it—"all free gratis"—and the goods, if any of us wished to get them for our own use, to go and get them, for "our father has given them to you."

Our chiefs began to think that Great Britain's king was very rich and powerful to force things in his domain, and kind to his nation, all things abundantly provided for his people and for us too. Several head of cattle were killed for us to eat, and flour provided. Our female party was very well pleased with the kindness we received from our white brethren.

Within two or three days—after our rest—the British commissioner visited us to make our acquaintance and to give us notice to meet together the following day at ten o'clock. When we went onto the ground of the council fire, he inquired whether all the chiefs of the Six Nations of the Indians were present.

Red Jacket said, "We are all supposed to be present, except the Onondaga chiefs, and we are ready to hear your proceeding."

The British commissioner now said, "I was sent by the father of Old England to communicate with the red brethren in regard to a quarrel which exists between the King of England's servants and America. This is the important point: we are bound to each other, each of the

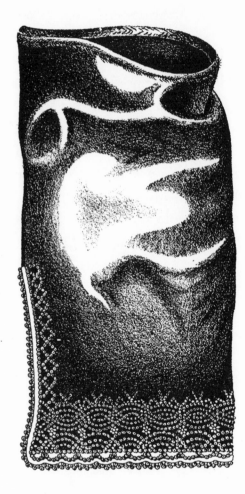

Female legging

two brothers, to help the other in any way and to love one another and be in good obedience and submission to the authority of our father who is able to support us when distressed. But here are the Americans, considered our father's children, but disobedient and rebellious to our father's rules and government.

"He therefore sent several of us to support our father's government. He wants you, all the Six Nations and other Indian nations, to turn out and join with him and give the Americans a dressing down and punishment for their disobedience and violating his laws. He calls upon you, all of the Six Nations and others who have not yet engaged to stand with their faces against their father's wishes, to turn out to correct the disobedient children.

"Our father will support you with all such necessary war utensils as guns and powder and lead and tomahawks and sharp edges [*knives and swords*]. And provisions and rations will be well supplied during this family quarrel. The father is rich. Everything is plentiful in his country.

"Now, the American is very poor; he has no means to force his business forward, and will soon give it up for he has no armorials [*weaponry*] to force against the British army. It is not only well armed, but has a great number of men to fight against

"The Commissioners [said] . . . that the king was rich and powerful . . . that his rum was as plenty as the water in Lake Ontario, that his men were as numerous as the sands upon the lakeshore . . ."
*Mary Jemison*

Stone tomahawk

America. The Americans, they cannot do anything against the British.

"Now here is your father, offering you his axe and tomahawk to hold against the Americans, and here is the butcher knife and Bowie knife [*anachronism; Jim Bowie, a hero of the Alamo, was born in 1796*] also, to take the American luck and scalps. And our father will pay so much for each scalp in money. But the American is very poor; he has no regular government.

"We will go from here to take all the forts belonging to America. Fort Stanwix we will take first and then Wyoming. These two forts that we will take will be sufficient to show our father's strength."

Joseph Brant, Cornplanter, Red Jacket, and several other chiefs and headmen of each nation of warriors agreed that they wanted to consider the subject. So they adjourned that day, until the next morning, that they might then be able to give an answer to all that had been laid before us. At that time, I felt desirous to know exactly what the general mind would be. As for my mind, I remembered the promise once made by the Six Nations to the Americans. I then supposed the chiefs would refuse the proposition of the redcoat man.

But the following day, at a meeting called by Brant and held amongst ourselves before the redcoat man called, Joseph Brant came forward and said that the offer was reasonable in all things, and that the King of Great Britain was the only father; if we rebelled and did nothing for him and likewise nothing for America, we would appear as though sleeping, all the chiefs and warriors, all except our womenfolk. They would be crying, and woe to us all, because there would be no peace for us anyhow, from either party, if we lay down and slept. We would be liable to have our throats cut by the redcoats or by the Americans.

"I say, take up the offer of the redcoat. I will urge my people to go and join the father, and help his people and his government. This is the only way for us. But every nation must speak for itself."

Red Jacket said, "I wish the warriors to have liberty to say something about this, for it's important, and any mistake may cost us our lives. I move for further consideration in regard to it. Our lives and property depend on this war."

Cornplanter said to his people, "Warriors, you must all mark and listen to what we have to say. War is war; death is the death; a fight is a hard business. Here is the American saying to us, not to lift our hands against either party—because they got into difficulty, it is nothing to us. He also says let him fight it out for his liberty and rebel against the government of his own brother. In fact, we the Indian nations of several different parts of this continent, we do not know what this war is for, and we are liable to make a mistake. I move that we wait a little while and hear more consultation. Let the British commissioner say all that he is going to say to us. We will then see clearly where we are going, for we are apt to be deceived."

Before Cornplanter finished speaking, Brant rose to his feet and said, "Nephew"—as he called Cornplanter according to their relationship—"stop speaking! You are a very cowardly man. It is hardly worthwhile to take notice of what you have said to our people. You have showed your cowardice." And Cornplanter said nothing more that day.

There was a great deal of controversy created amongst the warriors. Two parties formed—with some for Brant and some for Cornplanter. Red Jacket was there at the same time, but he did not say much of anything. It appeared that our brave warriors had not liked being called cowardly men. They began to say that we must fight for somebody and that they could not bear to be called cowards.

The British commissioner was now called into the council, and the warriors appeared to take more interest in his words.

"Brothers, our father in Old England loves you as well as the white people. He believes we are one, and all his children. He doesn't want any of the children to suffer, as I have said to you before. But I repeat, a part of the children have rebelled against the father's government, and he is going to correct the children who are now enemies to their father. And the Americans calculate to do more wrong to their father, and though they don't wish you to join with them, if you do, you may

depend upon it, you will lose
your country.

"We say, come, go along
with the father and he will
give you all you want—clothing and provisions—and to
your children and women
also, that they will not suffer
during the war with the

"Knee Rattles of deers'
hoofs . . . and in modern
times, of strips of metal, or of
bells, made a necessary part of
the costume [for the dance]."
*Lewis Henry Morgan*

rebellious children. These children will soon give it up
anyway, for they are poor and the father is very rich; his
goods are plentiful. Whatever you ask for, he will send
to you. Take them up now, take up the hatchet and sharp
edges and paint against the enemy! If you only obey
your father's wishes, you will have everything you need
to eat and drink, to wear, and money, too."

The warriors then proceeded to consider further and
consult together. There was speaking by brave warriors
then willing to go into the arrangement with the British.
Many of the warriors made different speeches on the

Knee rattle of deer hooves

"Wampum beads . . . are used chiefly for religious purposes and to preserve laws and treaties. They are made of the conch shell, which yields both a white and purple bead, the former of which is used for religious, and the latter for political purposes. A full string of wampum is usually three feet long, and contains a dozen or more strands. In ancient times, six of these strands was the value of a life, the amount paid in condonation of a murder. When sold, they were counted and reckoned at half a cent a bead. Wampum belts were made by covering one side of a deerskin belt with these beads, arranged after various devices, and with most laborious skill. A belt four or five feet long by four inches wide would require several thousands of these beads, they were estimated at great price."

*Lewis Henry Morgan*

subject of this warfare. However, they all seemed to want to do honor to their father. The old general [*probably loyalist Colonel John Butler*] made our people believe that we could not be defeated by the poor children of America.

The redcoat officers found that the warriors were split, and the party of women likewise. They began to use their influence over the warriors, and within about a day and a half, made considerable excitement amongst them by landing a ship at the mouth of Niagara Falls or at Fort Niagara. The ship brought in many small articles. It delivered small, jingling bells—and these were a curiosity to our women's eyes, as well as to their ears—and ostrich feathers.

The warriors also had never seen such things, and the articles were a curiosity to them, likewise, and the warriors were very well pleased with them. Beads were also delivered—to wear around the neck, and all were well pleased with these—and wonderful things to wear, and all these things were brought before us.

The British also brought over what they termed "wampum." They produced two ancient belts of wampum, so-called. One of twenty rows was called the "Old Covenant between the Indian Nations and the Whites." Whether this was so or not, I could tell nothing about it. But it did appear to me that the multitude of Indians believed most of what the British commissioner said to us.

The sachems gathered and consulted together on the important point: to which blood did we belong? Cornplanter did not wish to go to this meeting for many reasons.

The sachems then called on the Iroquois to give their

"...old John O'Bail, a white man...in his younger days had frequently passed through the Indian settlements that lay between the Hudson and Fort Niagara, and in some of his excursions had become enamored with a squaw, by whom he had a son that was called Cornplanter."
*Mary Jemison*

"...the Indian boys in the neighborhood . . . they took notice of my skin being of a different color from theirs, and spoke about it. I inquired of my mother the cause, and she told me that my father was a residenter [sic] in Albany . . . I grew up to be a young man, and married me a wife, and I had no kettle nor gun. I then knew where my father lived, and went to see him, and found he was a white man, and spoke the English language. He gave me victuals while I was at his house, but when I started home, he gave me no provision to eat on the way. He gave me neither kettle nor gun, neither did he tell me that the United States were about to rebel against the government of England . . ."
*Cornplanter*

earnest feelings on the whole matter laid before them, the subject of the warfare, and now we succeeded in bringing all to the council. Not a few spoke at that time, to the effect that the British government was very rich and kind to us and had made many attempts to show the good things they would do for us (because the father loved his red brethren and offered so many good things we had never seen before—the articles I've just been telling of—which looked well and considerable in my sight also). They therefore passed the resolution to take the King of England's men's offer to us. The majority of the Iroquois assented to hold faithful to the King; the mothers also assented.

"Women shall be considered the progenitors of the Nation. They shall own the land and the soil."

*The Constitution of the Five Nations*

Cornplanter spoke and said, "Every brave man show himself now, because hereafter we will encounter dangerous times during the action of the war. We will meet many a brave man amongst the American soldiers with their sharp-edged swords. I say you must stand like a good soldier against your own white brother, because just as soon as he finds out you are against him, he will show no mercy on you or on us. I say stand to your posts while there is still time, and be on your guard."

Brant was there all the time during the convention, and he all the time favored the British offer. And he used his influence to effect the wishes of the British government after our own convention adjourned, all through until the next day. On that day at the council ground, Joseph Brant said, "Our white brothers are now ready to hear us. I suppose our minds are all settled. I, therefore, am ready to answer and wish you all to say 'yes' or 'no.'" Almost everyone said "yes" at this time, and appeared willing.

Joseph Brant called to the British commissioner for order and said, "We, the Six Nations, have held a council by ourselves and taken a deep consideration of the war affair. Each nation has passed its own resolution in regard to it, and every one of the tribes assents to take up the offers you have made to us.

"We have communicated with the American commissioners about your brotherly difficulties; the Americans say the King of England has greatly misused America. If so, they do not deserve punishment. But we do not know what made the disturbance between you and America. We suppose it has to do with the arrangement between the two countries, which has not been settled and will not be settled.

"We, the Six Nations, now take up the offer—for we suppose America actually has disobeyed the father's laws, and so they deserve punishment. We will turn out and fight for the King for the father's sake, for we consider that he is the head man of all the nations of white people. We suppose you are one of his servants. Therefore, we will now take your hand for the bargain today.

"We may mistake the matter; we may be right or wrong. God, who regards us, knows. If we are on the right side, we will gain the day. But if we are on the wrong side, we will be defeated.

"Now it's your duty to give us instruction on the first course to take. We will do as you direct, for we think your protection is our protection. The bargain is made hand to hand. Though we are not sure we are right to agree to resolutions controlled by others' minds, we will now bind ourselves with the consent of a majority of our people."

The British commissioner—I don't know his name, although Brant called his name several times—answered, "Very good, Sir. Thank you all. We will firstly go to dinner and drink rum and sugar." And we did so that afternoon. Our head men drank a little too much rum; they did not do anything until the next morning, when we gathered again for instructions. The British commissioner said we must make preparations, gather ammunition and other military supplies. We would go first to attack Fort Stanwix and take that fort. If we met with good prospects there, we would go on to take Wyoming. That would be the second strike. When we had done both these things, the Americans might reconsider and surrender all at once. "But we will be with you at all times," said the redcoat man.

## CHAPTER THREE

# "Few White Men Escaped from Us"

At Oswego, Mohawk chief Joseph Brant assumed one of the two war leader positions traditionally held by the Seneca. With British support, he "bumped" the So No So Wa, then an aged chief known as Young King or Old Smoke. Cornplanter held the other head generalship. Brant or Thayendanegea (Mohawk for "bundle of sticks," meaning "strength") enjoyed many advantages because of his family relationship with the powerful Sir William Johnson. Brant had received an English education at missionary school in Connecticut, and then served a political and diplomatic apprenticeship under Sir William (who died in 1774). Brant visited London and the royal court in 1775 and aligned himself with the British cause after his return home. Brant did not share any blood or clan relationship with Cornplanter. At Oswego, he addressed Cornplanter as "Nephew," in a double-

*edged courtesy. It was polite to express a fictional family relationship, but not so polite to place the barely-younger Cornplanter in the subordinate role.*

We readied ourselves in a few days and met once again. The commander called everyone to order on the assembly ground and then set his big cannons to fire three times. All the captains and other officers brought out many good things in order to create good feelings amongst us, and they marched round several times when they were through.

The commander told us that we would go toward Fort Stanwix the next day, for we were ready to perform. We were instructed to go there, near the fort, and to wait for another army. So we started, all the warriors, and traveled several days before reaching the place appointed to stop. The British army reached it on the same day, so we were able to communicate with each other that evening.

In the morning, the first orders we had were to help the British build a thing of brush and trees to prevent the Americans from coming upon us in the night near Fort Stanwix; we went to work on

"The Commissioners made a present to each Indian of a suit of clothes, a brass kettle, a gun and tomahawk, a scalping knife, a quantity of powder and lead, a piece of gold . . . Many of the kettles which the Indians received at that time are now [1822] in use on the Genesee Flats."

*Mary Jemison*

War club

this. The British undertook to go into the fort to look over the situation and ascertain the number of them there and how the fort could be taken. Our British officer went to the American fort, pretending to seek the settlement of important affairs, but the object was to see what was going on inside the fort. But when our officer approached near to the gate of the fort, the enemy took him and blind-folded him, and then led him through the gate. He conversed with the [*American*] officers and stayed a quarter of an hour. When they let him out the gate, he informed us that the Americans would not surrender, but rather fight on and not give up the fort or their possessions. During this time, the Americans fired their cannon at us, and the British party began to fire at them.

While making preparation for battle, news came from the enemy that we must wait till they were ready. In about

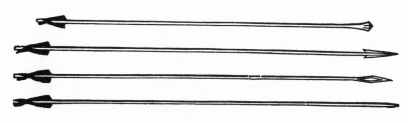

Arrows

"A few miles from the fort there was a deep ravine, sweeping toward the east in a semicircular form, and having a northern and southern direction. The bottom of this ravine was marshy, and the road along which the militia were marching crossed it by means of a log causeway. The ground thus partly enclosed by the ravine was elevated and level. Along the road, on each side on this height of land, Butler disposed his men.

"About ten o'clock on the morning of the 6th of August, the Tryon County militia arrived at this place without any suspicion of danger. The dark foliage of the forest trees, with a thick growth of underbrush, entirely concealed the enemy from their view. The advanced guard, with about two-thirds of the whole force, had gained the elevated ground; the baggage wagons had descended into the ravine . . . when the Indians arose, and with a dreadful yell poured a destructive fire upon them. The advanced guard was entirely cut off. Those who survived the first fire were immediately cut down with the tomahawk. The horror of the scene was increased by the personal appearance of the savages, who were almost naked and painted in the most hideous manner."

*Annals of Tryon County, account of the Battle of Oriskany*

two days, we received notice to take up arms, there were six thousand Americans arrived to meet us. Our chiefs' commander and other officers concluded we would march about three miles off from our camps to the chosen ground where we must shed our white brothers' blood and our own blood over the earth, and the bodies of the dead would be forever laid down—all for the cause of obtaining British government. The main object in going three miles off was to keep the stinking of the dead bodies from the tents.

So we marched out to the chosen ground, about the morning of the second day from the time our British officer was blindfolded before going into Fort Stanwix. We met the enemy near a small creek, where the six thousand men had cannon and we had none—just tomahawks and a few guns amongst us. But we agreed to fight with tomahawk and scalping knife. As we approached, we fired once and then ran amongst them. While doing so, it felt no more to me than to kill a beast. We killed most all of the Americans; only a few white men escaped from us there.

I saw many narrow places, and close to hand, where I might have been killed by the spear at the end of the musket.

Indian drum

"I saw some prisoners run the gauntlet. The Indian women and children formed two lines with clubs, stones, and whips in their hands. The prisoners would be started at the head of the lines and made to run through the whole length—the women and children pelting them as they ran."

*Jane Strope Whitaker, b. 1766, a captive of the Seneca in 1778–1780. She witnessed a milder gauntlet, not one composed of angry warriors.*

I had to defend myself with my hands and with acts of great exertion. There I saw, all over, the most dead bodies that I had ever seen—or ever would see, as I thought at that time. During the afternoon, blood was shed in a stream running down the descending ground. Some of the living cried for help, but I had no mercy to spare for them.

As to the distress of the Senecas, only thirty were killed at that time, and I took prisoners at that time, and some others took prisoners too. But they were killed by running through [*the gauntlet*] a certain distance, and not one escaped. They were

Deer-horn war club

all put to death in that way. We never undertook to bury them, so many of them. We only covered them up with brush, and after, we rested a little.

We met together with the British general. He informed us that Great Britain had sent a large army to assist us, a shipload of men for us, that they were coming upon the Mohawk River, and the British wanted us to go with them to meet those that were coming upon the river. So we went onto the bank of the river and stayed there a little while. Then the general ordered us to go home and see our families. We returned for our families by orders of the British general. In traveling home, we took considerable care to avoid trouble and avoid Fort Stanwix for fear that we might be attacked without warning.

"Previous to the battle at Fort Stanwix, the British sent for the Indians to come and see them whip the rebels, and at the same time stated that they did not wish to have them fight, but wanted to have them just sit down, smoke their pipes and look on. Our Indians went, to a man; but contrary to their expectation, instead of smoking and looking on, they were obliged to fight for their lives . . . with a great loss in killed and wounded. Our Indians alone had thirty-six killed and a great number wounded. Our town exhibited a scene of real sorrow and distress. The mourning was excessive and was expressed by the most doleful yells, shrieks, and howlings."
*Mary Jemison*

## CHAPTER FOUR

# "It Was Done in Honor"

T he grand British strategy of 1777 failed. Burgoyne met defeat at Saratoga, thirty miles north of Albany; Howe remained bottled up in Philadelphia; and though "few white men escaped" from Chainbreaker and his allies at Oriskany, St. Leger withdrew without taking Fort Stanwix. Both sides claimed victory at Oriskany, and both sides lost many men. The battle broke the political unity of the Iroquois Confederacy. Seneca, Mohawk, and Cayuga fought and died there with the British. Thus, they separated themselves from the Oneida and Tuscarora, who, under the influence of New England missionaries, held to the rebel colonists' cause. In a further split, the greater part of the Onondaga Nation remained strictly neutral.

We kept right on annoying our enemies till we had a battle, or rather, destroyed a town near to and on the west side of Albany. This was in the spring of the year 1778. At this time, I was chosen to take charge of a certain army of the Indians. My father had been one of the Seneca chiefs killed by the American warriors immediately after the Fort Stanwix battle on one of the branches of the Mohawk River, where my father's bones now remain. All his men and Uncle Cornplanter having so much confidence in me, a noted young man, they gave me an office or something to do over the people at that time. My mother was then living, and she married a few years after my father was killed; she married a man by the name of Jackson and bore a boy by him. My mother lived twenty years after my father's death in 1777.

In the summer of the year 1777, I made the first move to go and attack an American fort, which the Indians called Fort Gah Doh Ga—the English name I did not know. We had a good fight there and used the means which we had used before in battle. As I said before, we had not permission to fire guns, but only to use the knife and tomahawk and run right amongst them and cut men down. I killed—how many I could not tell, for I paid no attention nor kept an account of it. It was a great many. But I never have, at any of my battles, thought about keeping account of the number I killed at one time. But I have thought of it often since, that it was very sinful in the sight of God. Oh, I do think so! It is bad enough to spill human blood! But again, I have thought that it was done in honor to protect our own country where all the Indian nations were built forever.

We retreated for the winter in the year 1777–78. We placed ourselves near home for our hunting till spring. We readied ourselves to hunt deer, bear, elk, and other game for provisions, preparing for the next season of war and for our children and old folks, for whom we have to provide all their wants. We always make such preparations before we leave them.

". . . the mother of the young warrior returned a present of venison, or other fruit of the chase, to the mother of the bride, as an earnest of his ability to provide for his household."

*Lewis Henry Morgan*

About the month of March, several of us made a journey home from hunting. On the way home, we made a stop three miles from Genesee Falls, near the

Headdress

bank of the Genesee River, to make our dinner with the dried venison which we carried in our baggage. We struck a fire to cook the venison, and during the building of the fire, I took my gun and stepped out upon the bank of the river that I might find some waterfowl to shoot at. My object was to save the feathers for headdresses or for making a crown to wear on my head when enjoying myself at home.

I was about eighty rods [*a rod equals five and a half yards*] from where we had all stopped, when I heard someone whistle or make some such sound on my left side, within a few rods of me. I listened for some time, but heard no more. I wheeled back toward our fire, till I came within ten rods of our folks, or near enough so some of them saw me coming toward them. I then heard the sound again—right behind

"Upon the head-dress, Gus-to-weh . . . much attention was bestowed. The frame consisted of a band of splint, adjusted around the head, with a cross-band arching over the top, from side to side. A cap of net-work, or other construction, was then made to enclose the frame. Around the splint, in later times, a silver band was fastened, which completed the lower part. From the top, a cluster of white feathers depended. Besides this, a single feather of the largest size, was set in the crown of the head-dress, inclining backwards from the head. It was secured in a small tube, which was fastened to the cross-splint, and in such a manner as to allow the feather to revolve in the tube. This feather, which was usually the plume of the eagle, is the characteristic of the Iroquois head-dress."

*Lewis Henry Morgan*

"Some of the feather headdresses of the warriors were very imposing, waving above the top of the head. They were generally eagles' feathers. Others inclined upon the side, tied with cord and tapels."

*Jane Strope Whitaker*

me. I turned and looked backward; as soon as I turned, they [*the hidden enemy*] fired at me. But not any one of them touched me with their bad [*musket*] balls. When, after they fired, I saw twenty-five or thirty men, some well armed, I just gave the war whoop and made a jump toward them. I ran with all my might and pursued them.

My gun lock struck on the limb of a tree and broke, so my gun was good for nothing, though still kept in my hand. The enemy fired once more before I overtook them. The first one, I came to him, and he wheeled round about and drew his sword and was going to lay it over me. I lifted up my gun barrel; he struck that and broke it in two. In this moment, I took him as my prisoner and took his arms and ammunition away from him. Another Indian brother came upon the run; I told him to take this prisoner, and he did so.

I had pursued the first man for one mile, now I ran another mile to overtake three other white men, running before me. I hallooed [*shouted*] to

"All the prisoners that are taken in battle and carried to the encampment or town by the Indians, are given to the bereaved families, till their number is made good. And unless the mourners have but just received the news of their bereavement, and are under the operation of a paroxysm of grief, anger and revenge; or, unless the prisoner is very old, sickly, or homely, they generally save him, and treat him kindly. But if their mental wound is fresh, their loss so great that they deem it irreparable, or if their prisoner or prisoners do not meet with their approbation, no torture, let it be ever so cruel, seems sufficient to make them satisfaction."

*Mary Jemison*

them. They found me alone; they spun right round about and discharged their guns at me. I do not know where their [*musket*] balls went or what became of them, but they never touched me. In a moment, the three men might have killed me—just as well as not—for I found they were too many to stand against. I felt Death. Yet, I made the Indian whoop and also made signs as though somebody was with me, nearby, and other signs as I was approaching them, that if they gave up their arms and ammunition, they would save their lives. And they did so, when I came to them.

At this time, I had nothing but the tomahawk, nothing beneficial to defend myself with. But I took one by his arm and one by his hands, and told them they were prisoners and must go along with me. Three other Indians came to us and I told them these three white men would be saved. But one man refused to go. The other two, they advised him to go with them. He talked to them a while. I did not learn what he said to them, but when I told him to come right along, he shook his head and made a sign that he would rather die. I felt sorrow for him; I wanted him the best of the three. But he again made the sign that he would rather die than go, and I said to the Indians that they must kill him. We took the two other men back with us, about three miles, to our camp, where we ate a little. We then picked up our baggage and went down the river a half a mile to a place where you could build a float to cross the river, for the river was considerably high. So we went at it and built a couple of them to carry all of us, the twenty men of our party, in

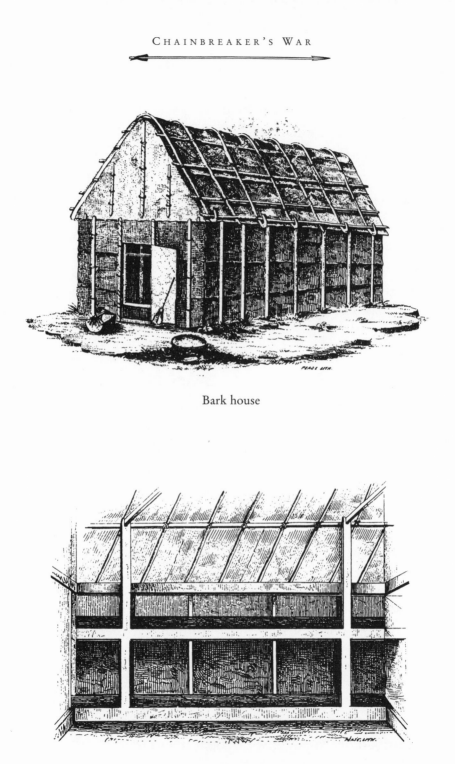

Bark house

Interior view of bark house

"The Ga-no-sote, or Bark-house, was a simple structure. When single, it was about twenty feet by fifteen upon the ground, and from fifteen to twenty feet high . . . In the centre of the roof was an opening for the smoke, the fire being upon the ground in the centre of the house, and the smoke ascending without the guidance of a chimney . . . Within, upon the two sides, were arranged wide seats, also of bark boards, about two feet from the ground, well supported underneath, and reaching the entire length of the house. Upon these they spread their mats of skins, and also their blankets, using them as seats by day and couches at night. Similar berths were constructed on each side, about five feet above these, and secured to the frame of the house, thus furnishing accomodations for the family. Upon cross-poles, near the roof, was hung, in bunches, braided together by husks, their winter supply of corn. Charred and dried corn and beans were generally stored in bark barrels, and laid away in corners . . . After they had learned the use of the axe, they began to substitute houses of hewn logs, but they constructed them after the ancient model."

*Lewis Henry Morgan*

"A rough shelf at one end held a small brass kettle, a few bark trays and several short square-edge wooden spoons. Pegs in the front wall supported a rifle and its equipments, a tomahawk and other articles, the property of the husband. In one corner, near the door, stood an ax, a hollow block of wood and a pestle for pounding corn, the implements of the wife . . . three or four flat smooth stones frequently used for baking, were half hidden in the bed of ashes [of the fireplace]."

***Life of Horatio Jones.*** *Jones, 1762–1836, was captured by Seneca warriors in 1778.*

crossing the river. We crossed safely and went about one mile from the river, where we retired for the night after arranging for regular watches. We sent watches back to the river to see whether our enemy had pursued our track during the night.

Toward morning, the men of the watch discovered firelight below us on the other side of the river. About breaking daylight, we made a start, along with the three prisoners. We traveled on very fast and kept three Indians as far as a half mile behind us, for fear that our enemy continued to follow us.

We traveled all day, and made no stops. We traveled for some time after dark to get in as far as we could. When we came to stop, we made no fire, just laid right down. The night was favorable without fire; we covered ourselves up with skins and furs and laid very comfortably through the night. In the morning, we started on, expecting that we would be at home about noon. We carried dried venison with us that could be eaten as we went along without stopping, for fear our enemy might overtake their "pursuers."

The first house we came to, there we found only old folks, the old squaw and the old man. The young Indian was gone away from home, and the boys also, and the young squaw also was gone.

I thought we had escaped from the enemy after we got home. But soon, we heard that the old folk had been murdered by the Yankees. The old squaw, they took her scalp and went off with it. I then supposed that the enemy must have kept very close to our heels, although we escaped from them. No longer after we got home than it takes a man to fill up a pipe with his tobacco and smoke it up, we heard that the old folks were murdered—by those who followed us, I felt no doubt about it.

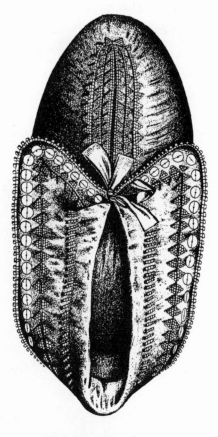

Woman's moccasin

The three prisoners that we brought home with us, I secured them well. And ten of us put out and pursued those who had murdered the old folks, as far as we could track them. In the night, rain came and it grew so dark that we could not go on. We stopped for that night, which was very wet, till the next morning. We could not track them any more and were obliged to quit them and go back. When we reached home once more, there we saw another family all killed—by whom we could not learn, only we supposed this must have been done in the night.

All the tracks we could find were "barefooted," but for one. About half a mile distant, I found a shoe track. I said to my men that I had found the white men's track and that they must have been the ones who murdered the family that night. White men wear shoes; the Indians wear moccasins. By these, it is generally very easy to tell the white tracks from Indian ones. I therefore was well convinced that white warriors had murdered this family. We were obliged to set watches or guard stations in different places every night for some time, so that they did not come any more.

Man's moccasin

CHAPTER FIVE

# "I Killed Many"

Throughout 1778, Seneca warriors took part in raids on rebel settlements and small forts in frontier regions of New York and Pennsylvania. Fort Niagara served as the British center of operations in this border war, and Joseph Brant and Loyalist Colonel John Butler acted as the chief strategists. The attack on Wyoming, Pennsylvania, on July 1–3 was one of the most successful of these raids. The Battle of Wyalusing on September 29, also fought in Pennsylvania, was a different kind of action. There, the Seneca and others sought to punish American raiders led by Colonel Thomas Hartley (not General James Potter, as Chainbreaker supposes).

About three months after this, we were to go with an army of three hundred men commanded by General Duckey, as we called this British officer [*Colonel John Butler's son, Captain Walter Butler, whose Iroquois nickname was "Dux E A," or "Leader"*]. Or rather, we had notice to be ready at such a time and to meet with them at such a place and on such a day. There, arrangements were to be made and instructions given us on what we would perform at the place called by the Indians, Da A I Dah A. I did not know the English name of this town where we were going to fight.

When the time of our appointment arrived, we were ready and met with General Duckey and his army. We were to go on one side of the town or village, and they were to go on the other side of said village. They were to attack first and draw the enemy's attention from us so we could come behind the enemy's hills and put our tomahawks on the back sides of their heads. And this was the understanding so agreed.

We departed; one party went on one route and the other went on a different route. But somehow, we reached there first, about two hours before them. When we sent to the village for a report, we did not receive any report until two hours after the time we first sent for it. The report was that we must now go near to the village and watch for opportunity, according to the understanding. As we arrived there, the fight had commenced on the other side of the village. We did not have any opportunity

"My mother and her six children, including myself, were made captives by the Indians on the 20th day of May previous to the massacre [Wyoming]. My grandparents and three sisters of my mother who had come with my father from Catskill, walking their families into the settlement, were all captured. The capture was in the morning; we were all at breakfast. The Indians numbered thirteen with three squaws in their company. I think they were Senecas; they came from the Genesee. They took as at once to Tioga Point. There they gave us up to Butler at the head of his Rangers, composed of Indians and British soldiers . . .

While at Tioga, we picked our living from the fields and woods—strawberries, raspberries, and later in the season blackberries. The Indians did not abuse us, except that they gave us no bread or salt . . . Before embarking in their canoes for Wyoming, the Indians streaked their faces with black paint put on in stripes, also with a yellowish red paint. After they were all ready, they stood up in the backs of their canoes and sung war songs. I heard them speak of killing white dogs, roasting them, and each warrior partaking, both before and after the Wyoming Battle."

*Jane Strope Whitaker*

to see; we only heard the gunfire and the halloos [*shouts*]. I said to my men that we would never do anything, else we went that moment. I gave orders to march on and run and take all alive, if possible, and to show our bravery. I gave them good encouragement. So started, I said nothing more until we came through the battle.

As for myself—what I did during the actions of this battle—I started from the same point as all the rest, but I

"Frequent rumors reached us that the enemy meditated an attack upon our homes at Wyoming, which we were raised to defend. Our officers petitioned to be sent there, but Congress and his excellency could not let us go. At length the danger became so imminent, and the entreaties from home so pressing, that many obtained furloughs to return. Congress consolidated the two companies into one, under Captain Spaulding, and detached it for Wyoming; but it got there too late. Some few of the officers, Lieutenant Pearce among the number, by riding all night through the wilderness, got in just time enough to die on the field..."

*George Ransom, b. 1763, Pennsylvania militiaman*

"On the day of the battle... [I] could hear the savage whoop begin on one end of the line, and, being taken up and repeated, run, whoop after whoop, then yell after yell, from one end to the other. It was a mournful sound and boded ill to our people."

*Bertha Jenkins, b. 1754, resident of Wyoming*

did not see them for some time after I ran into the village amongst them. The first man I came to, I fired at him and killed him. But with the next one, I just laid the butt end of my gun over his head; down he went. I minded no more about him—expected he was dead. With the third one, I took him the same way, and thought I might take his scalp. As I drew my knife to his head, and looking back, I saw the other man that I had "butted" over, come to me and draw his gun and point it toward me. But as he fired, an Indian came up behind him, and I sprang at him and gave the war whoop. He just touched my clothes with his [*musket*] ball, never drew any blood out of me. I had my knife in hand; I drew it upon his throat and cut it. Down he went the second time; I said to myself, "Now, I guess he will stay down!"

I ran and saw a couple of Indians wounded; they were

Knee band

Wrist band

Arm band

"Early the next morning we could see them fixing their scalps on little bows made of small sticks, and, with their moccason awls and a string, were sewing them round the bows, and scraping off the flesh and blood, carefully drying them, and at the same time smoking."

*Elisha Harding, b. circa 1760, Pennsylvania militiaman*

"The battlefield presented a distressing sight; in a ring, round a rock, there lay 18 or 20 mangled bodies. Prisoners taken on the field . . . [had been] placed in a circle surrounded by Indians, and a squaw set to butcher them."

*George Ransom*

unable to go on. I ran on farther and told other Indians to go back and take care of them, and they did so. I went to another street where there was more for me to do. I just took my tomahawk and struck one and then another and so on. I didn't mind anything about the crying women and children—or the men, some just dying, some fighting, and in every kind of shape. There were not many guns fired in that fight, and it lasted a great while. I do not know how many I killed, only that I killed many, and that I came through very narrow places where I might have been killed myself.

When we finished fighting, we gathered together, and General Duckey ordered us to go and destroy all the village—for the people, they were almost destroyed any-

Various forms of hulling baskets

way—and take the goods and cattle, horses and sheep, and whatever provisions, and take all along, and by this means subdue them so that they would never rise up again. There were very few who escaped from us at that time, and those had all their property taken by the whites. But as for myself, as for taking kinds of property, I did not, because I thought it bad enough to kill men and destroy their village. The bodies were laid out there when we came away from this place. No prisoners [*of the combatants*] had been saved,

" . . . prisoners were kept at the fort 7 or 8 days; squaws would come over with scalps of our people strung together, and worn as a band round their waist; they [the prisoners] were then all sent off; about 60 started together, and as if there was some touch of mercy left, they let them take a cow or two; fires were burning all around them; their houses were burned and harvest lost . . . the distress no tongue can tell. If a few were left no one could tell why."

*Ishmael Bennett, b. 1762, resident of Wyoming*

and the children, a few, were left. I know not what became of them. We left them there, uncared for, just as the General ordered us to do no more.

We went back home to the Genesee River near Canawagus. We reached home about the time to harvest

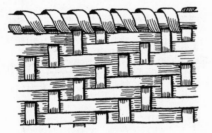

Hulling basket detail

"After they [the Delaware] had been subdued, and had acknowledged their dependence by sending the tributary wampum, they made an inroad upon a western nation under the protection of the Iroquois . . . A deputation of Iroquois chiefs went immediately into the country of the Delawares, and having assembled the people in council, they degraded them from the rank of even a tributary nation . . . they forbade them from ever after going out to war, divested them of all civil powers, and declared that they should henceforth be as women . . . putting upon them the Ga-ka-ah, or skirt of the female, and placing in their hands a corn-pounder . . ."

*Lewis Henry Morgan*

what little corn had been planted by our squaws and children.

We stayed at home peaceably all the fall and winter till the spring of 1779. At that time, we had small battles, with a few of us sometimes going off to small settlements and villages where we used to go and fight. We always had the advantage over the people there and killed them, as many as we could, which was considerable. By and by, the British officer would call us to go to a certain place with him and his small company.

We did this often, till we heard from a messenger, sent from the Delaware Nation of the Susquehanna, that the American troops were coming to destroy the Delaware tribes. They wished us to protect them, at very short notice, and put us to a great deal of trouble in our minds, for we didn't have time enough to send a messenger to call upon General Duckey and Joseph Brant. Both were at Fort Niagara. This made us feel very unhappy.

But Cornplanter, and Red Jacket, and myself, Chainbreaker, Captain Pollard, and Young King, and

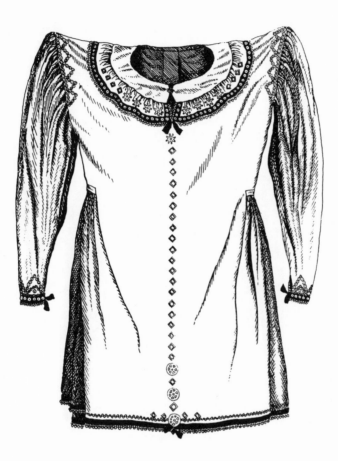

Over-dress front

several other chiefs of the Six Nations put heads together
and consulted in regard to this notice. We agreed that we
would go and assist the Delaware, that we would do all
we could for them to save their nation. On short notice,
we gathered together one thousand men, Indians only,
and brave men all of them. We had to go without General
Duckey and Brant, or any of those from headquarters,

Over-dress back

and we felt destitute of provisions and other means. But we all agreed that we would go.

We started on the run, part of the way, in order to meet General Potter [*Brigadier General James Potter, 1729–89*] at Wyoming [*Wyalusing*] in Pennsylvania. We endeavored to get there in time; we traveled five days on the way before we arrived among the Delaware settlements.

We then learned that Potter had three thousand men with him, and we were only about fourteen hundred to stand against Potter of the three thousand men, and well-armed men, too. So we consulted together about this — what course we would take. We finally found we could not avoid it, that we must stand

" . . . the War Chief shall sing the War Song as he approaches the country of the enemy and not cease until his scouts have reported that the army is near the enemies' lines."
*The Constitution of the Five Nations*

and fight, or surrender. So we appointed the commanders and captains, and all came to bind themselves, one to the other, to fight with tomahawks and to fight till all were killed. None bound themselves that night, because we were afraid. But after meeting in council and encouraging one another, early in the morning, all were ready to go to the chosen ground, where we calculated to make contact with the three thousand men.

It was supposed a messenger's report might be received from General Potter, and we waited for it for some time. It did not come, so we went onto the ground. The moment we appeared, Potter began to fire upon us and command his troops to close with us. When they fired, I commanded a chase [*charge*] of the warriors. I gave the war whoop and orders to go in amongst the enemy — just to fire once and then run in. The way we slew them was wicked. But I felt no mercy. We just wielded the tomahawks and knives and swords with all our might.

Corn mortar

The action of fighting commenced about nine o'clock AM and lasted till two in the afternoon. We could only tell our own party by the marks on our hands and on our faces. But we feared nothing. I thought to die there; it was as good a place as any other. It was a very hard fight for four hours. Potter began to retreat, and at that time, I slew more than at other times in this action. After the battle was over, we supposed two thousand of the Americans had been killed and the rest had run. We never left any wounded, but killed them as we went along. Only those who were able to run, they escaped. Of the Six Nations, five were killed and a great many wounded. At that time, we did not use guns much. Mostly we used tomahawks and swords. The way we used to do was to go and run amongst them and give them no chance to fire their guns. As for myself, I took my tomahawk and sword and went amongst the enemy and knocked down and cut with my sword and cut men down—two and more as I went by.

After the battle, blood showed spilled on the ground—more than I ever did see. At this time, we took the bodies and buried as many as we could—commenced to bury them with branches and other stuff to cover the bodies. The next morning, we had trouble in burying the dead bodies, which we were gathering into heaps. We did not know which bodies were which at that time.

"They are a strange enemy, they shun Danger when among us, but near their own country, they fight brave."

*Colonel Thomas Hartley, American commander at Wyalusing*

Cornplanter, and Red Jacket, and Young King, and myself, and all the leading men of the Six Nations were present at this battle. Only Joseph Brant was not there.

## CHAPTER SIX

# "The Danger Was Near at Hand"

In 1779, the Continental Congress and George Washington decided to move in force against the hostile Iroquois. In April, Colonel Daniel Brodhead raided and burned Onondaga villages on one of the New York branches of the Susquehanna River. (The Americans suspected the Onondaga of aiding Seneca war parties.) In August, Brodhead led an eight-hundred-man force north along the Allegheny to attack Seneca territory. At the same time, two separate, fifteen-hundred-man American armies ravaged Mohawk settlements along the Mohawk and Susquehanna rivers, then joined forces under the command of Major General John Sullivan to head west across the Finger Lakes. Thus, the Seneca faced a second, massive attack from Sullivan.

Chainbreaker may refer to the Battle of Newtown, August 29, when he says, "We divided our men—some went upon the

hill." *But it's more likely that all of the narrative here relates to
an encounter at Conesus—not Seneca—Lake.*

About the spring of the year
1779, some of our men were
out east, hunting, and they
came across American troops coming
on toward the Genesee River to
attack the Six Nations. According to
the tidings they brought us, the troops would not be able
to reach the river for five days; they calculated the trouble
the Americans would have to move through the wilderness with their arms and ammunition. At this time,
Joseph Brant was at Fort Niagara in council with the
British officers. We did not have time to send to Brant and
others for assistance and protection. We had to stand our
own ground and make preparation to meet the enemy.

The watch men told us that the enemy were coming to
a certain place. We started with three hundred men early
in the morning. We traveled on toward Seneca Lake all
day; we did not reach there till the next day at noon.
When we came to Seneca Lake, we divided our men—
some went upon the hill. When we ascended to the top of
the hill, we saw the American troops coming on toward
the other company. We then immediately marched down
hill to meet our men. After descending, we saw the
Americans had even more men than we were aware of. So
we concluded to stand back, for we were not able to stand
against them till we had a better chance. The Americans
fired their guns and cannon at us, but we stood back and

kept running till night. We then retired for the night; the American troops retired for the night about one mile from us, their general not known to us by name. In the morning, the American warriors approached toward us and fired at us. We began to wake and to cheer up; we started to approach them. Within a half mile, we came to a small swamp, and we saw the enemy coming on, a great

"Our Indians . . . became alarmed and suffered every thing but death from fear that they should be taken by surprize, and totally destroyed at a single blow. But in order to prevent so great a catastrophe, they sent out a few spies who were to keep themselves at a short distance in front of the invading army . . ."
*Mary Jemison*

body of men. We were frightened then, and we wheeled right back again through this little swamp and stopped on the far edge.

The enemy after us thought that they had to cut a road through this swamp. So we stood a proper distance away from where they came out of the swamp. While we stood there, we saw fifty men of the enemy coming behind us. Some of the Indian companies hallooed to the headquarters to fire at once. Then we ran against them and went amongst them with force and slew them with tomahawk and swords, and destroyed them all. An Oneida Indian amongst the whites' army, we took him prisoner for a few minutes. One of the Seneca chiefs slew him with a tomahawk, killed him, because this Oneida had an Indian scalp tied on his belt—consequently his life was not spared.

"[Sept. 13, 1779] . . .
reached a town . . . called
Koneghsaws. Here we found
some large corn fields which
part of the army destroyed
while the other part were
employed in building a bridge
. . . I had the preceding evening
ordered out an officer with
three or four riflemen, one of
our guides and an Oneida chief
to reconnoitre the Chinesee
[Genesee] town, that we might,
if possible, surprise it.
Lieutenant Boid was the officer
entrusted with this service, who
took with him twenty-three
men, volunteers from the same
corps, and a few from Colonel
Butler's regiment, making in all
twenty-six . . . they saw a few
Indians, killed and scalped two
. . . but soon found themselves
almost surrounded by three or
four hundred Indians and
rangers. Those of Mr. Boid's
men who were sent to secure his
flanks fortunately made their
escape; but he with fourteen of
his party and the Oneida chief
being in the centre were completely encircled."

*Major General John Sullivan*

After this, we went on toward the head of Seneca Lake; a few Indian families lived there. But we found them all killed by the whites; here, I suppose, the Oneida Indian had taken his scalp. We passed along toward Geneseo and came out to the river at the place now called Mount Morris. There, twenty-five hundred men of the Six Nations stood ready to meet the Americans and to have a battle. But the Americans went back toward New York, so we did not have any fight there.

While we were gone to Wyoming and other places to war against our own American white brothers, Captain Red Eyes and other Indians with Red Eyes, about ten of them, followed the Allegheny River downstream in bark canoes, hunting for furs. Red Eyes and his comrades were down about five miles below Broken Straw in what is now Warren County, Pennsylvania. They had camped out on the bank of the river, when Captain Red Eyes took his rifle and walked along the bank about a quarter of a mile from his camp. There, he saw a company of men and counted them—how many were in the company. There were about five hundred men; they saw him and he ran back to his camp. They fired at him, but the musket balls didn't touch him, and he ran as fast as he could. They put out after him, about fifty of them, but he rather outran them.

As soon as he reached camp, he told his comrades that the whites' company was close at hand, that they had better run. So they started and ran for their lives. Some ran up the river, and Red Eyes and three others who went with him took their bark canoe to put across the river. But before reaching across, the company came upon them and fired, and those three Indians were killed in the river, while crossing.

"At that time, I had three children who went with me on foot, one who rode on horseback, and one whom I carried on my back . . . In one or two days after the skirmish at Connissius Lake, Sullivan arrived at Genesee River, where they destroyed every article of the food kind that they could lay their hands on. A part of our corn they burnt, and threw the remainder into the river. They burnt our houses, killed what few cattle and horses they could find, destroyed our fruit trees, and left nothing but the bare soil and timber.

". . . we hunted continually till . . . we all returned; but what were our feelings when we found that there was not a mouthful of any kind of sustenance left, not even enough to keep a child one day from perishing with hunger."
*Mary Jemison*

"I left this place [Pittsburgh] the 11th of last month [August, 1779] with six hundred & five Rank & File ... on the march for Canawago on the path leading to Cuscushing; at ten miles on this side the town ... discovered between thirty & Forty warriors coming down the Allegheny River in seven Canoes. These warriors having likewise discovered some of the Troops, immediately landed stript off their shirts & prepared for action, and the advanced Guard immediately began the attack—All the troops except one column & Flankers being in the narrows between the River and high hill were immediately prepared to receive the enemy, which being done, I went forward to discover the Enemy, & six of them retreating over the River without arms, at the same time the rest ran away leaving their Canoes, Blankets, Shirts, provision and eight Guns, besides five dead and by the signs of Blood, several went off wounded, only two of my men & one of the Delaware Indians (Narrowland) were wounded ..."

*Colonel Daniel Brodhead*

Red Eyes jumped out of the canoe into the water and dove in the water as far as he could go under. The company kept firing guns at him as long as they could see him, but he made it across the river alive. As soon as he came out of the water, he ran to the first tree and hid behind that till the water drained from him, and he made his escape from them—though the whites' company kept pursuing him up the river.

Captain Red Eyes kept going day and night until he came up to what is now called Cornplanter's Reservation [*Burnt House, Pennsylvania*]. At that time and at that place, there was no regular settlement, only a few Indian families had stopped there to raise some corn in the year 1779. The Indians and women and children prepared themselves to leave, away from the danger of their enemy coming up the river. Red Eyes urged his people to ready themselves, and then made all the Indians march up the river. They took baggage with some provisions and venison, and the young ones, and carried them away as soon as possible. For the danger was near at hand. The five hundred men were coming to destroy them.

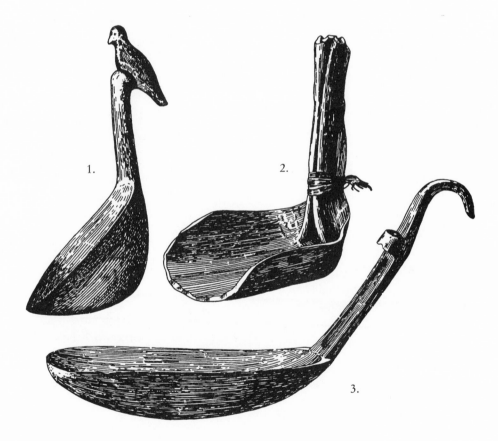

Types of Seneca and Onondaga eating spoons:
1. wooden spoon; 2. bark ladle; 3. buffalo horn spoon

"Some of them fled just before the advanced Guards reached the Towns & left several packs of Deer skins. At the upper Seneca Towns we found a painted image or War post, clothed in Dog skin, & John Montour told me this Town was called Yoghroonwago, besides this we found seven other Towns, consisting in the whole of one hundred and thirty Houses, some of which were large enough for the accomodation of three or four Indian families. The Troops remained on the ground three whole days destroying the Towns & Corn Fields. I never saw finer Corn altho' it was planted much thicker than is common with our Farmers . . . the plunder is estimated at 30 m. [30,000] Dollars."

*Colonel Daniel Brodhead*

So they got away and left all those immoveables—such as crops in the ground—and came into the State of New York and made a stop at what is now Cold Spring, New York. They retired there for a few days and immediately sent a messenger over to the Genesee River and to headquarters [*Fort Niagara*] to let them know about the disturbances and about the persons killed at the time Red Eyes had been driven from hunting. When Red Eyes first reached Cold Spring, his company buried their corn and venison under the ground. You have seen the holds [*caches*] frequently alongside the river—like potato holds—where the Indians buried their provisions and cooking

Wooden spoon

utensils when they were wandering about in the woods and forests till Uncle Cornplanter, Red Jacket, and myself came over to protect them.

When we came down to Cornplanter's Reservation in Pennsylvania where Red Eyes had his corn that season, the whites had been there and cut all the corn and thrown it in the river so that they could not have any. The whites had gone down again; we pursued them as far as Warren, Pennsylvania, and saw nothing of them. So we returned and called upon all the Indians and went far upstream, and then over to the Genesee River, and down home again to Canawagus before the winter set in.

A few days afterward, a messenger arrived from Fort Niagara. Word was sent to us that a display of war plans was to take place. We then held a general council of the Six Nations to calculate what

"The Iroquois were accustomed to bury their surplus corn and also their charred green corn in caches, in which the former would preserve uninjured through the year, and the latter for a much longer period. They excavated a pit, made a bark bottom and sides, and having deposited their corn within it, a bark roof, water tight, was constructed over it, and the whole covered with earth . . . Cured venison and other meats were buried in the same manner, except that the bark repository was lined with deer-skins."

*Lewis Henry Morgan*

"My brothers understood the customs of the Indians when they were obliged to fly from their enemies, and suspecting that their corn, at least, must have been hid, made diligent search, at length found a large quantity of it, together with beans, sugar, and honey, so carefully buried that it was completely dry and as good as when they left it."

*Mary Jemison, relating her account of a journey in the 1760s*

Bowl

"For bread, purple calico and the two hominy corns were used . . . the meal was mixed with boiling water and quickly molded into a flattened cake about eight inches in diameter and 3 inches thick. The cake was then plunged into boiling water and cooked for nearly an hour. The object of mixing the meal with boiling water was to coagulate the starch and make the meal stick together . . . when the loaf floats it is considered properly cooked. Sometimes the molded loaf is baked instead of boiled, specially for journeys. The loaf is buried in hot ashes and a roaring fire built over it until it is baked thoroughly. When it is to be eaten the ashes are washed off . . ."

*Arthur C. Parker, 1881–1955, anthropologist and member of the Seneca Nation*

course we would pursue. The resolution was to go to Fort Niagara in order to find out the plans of the War Department. It was unanimously agreed in this council that I, Chainbreaker, and Uncle Cornplanter, and other chief commanders of the armies of the Six Nations, and the warriors would all go to Fort Niagara. This was in the fall of the year 1779. Every man took his knapsack with Indian bread calculated to last on the away journey toward Fort Niagara.

Our families were left at home on the Genesee River, and part of the warriors stayed for the protection of those at home, and the rest of us all went to Fort Niagara. I saw nothing on my journey worthy of saying anything about.

When we arrived at Fort Niagara, Joseph Brant was there and all the generals and other officers in the wars. I immediately visited the Onondagas. This was immediately after the corn harvest, when I arrived at the Onondagas. I saw but a few Onondaga Indians. They were almost all gone, taken as prisoners by white people in force, and taken to Fort Stanwix. One Indian's family was destroyed entirely, and the Indians' town was burnt. A few Indians escaped at the time the others were taken. I called them together for the purpose of obtaining information from them concerning this affair of the war—for I knew that the Onondaga stood neutral, not taking the part of either party, and I wished to learn all the circum-

Ft. Niagara: "... a large fort with bastions and ravelins, ditches and pickets, curtains and counter-scarp, covered way, draw-bridge, raking batteries, stone towers, bakery, blacksmith shop, mess-house, barracks, laboratory, magazine, and a chapel with a dial over its door to mark the progress of the hours. It covered about eight acres. A few rods from the barrier-gate was a burial ground, over the portal of which was painted in large letters, REST. The dungeon of the mess-house, called the black hole was a strong, dark, and dismal place ..."

***Pictorial Fieldbook of the Revolution***

"There civilized Europe reveled with savage America, and ladies of education and refinement mingled in the society of those whose only distinction was to wield the bloody tomahawk and the scalping knife. There the squaws of the forests were raised to eminence, and the most unholy unions between them and officers of the highest rank smiled upon and countenanced."

***Falls of Niagara***

"21st [April, 1779] . . . came to Onandaga creek, small but deep, had to cross it on a log. Capt. Grahams Co Just as he had crossed the creek caught an Indian who was shooting Pidgeons & made him prisoner, And we got some information from him, then proceeded on till we come within about one Mile of the Town when we recd. Word from Capt. Graham that he had caught one Squaw and killed one and had taken two or three children and one White man and one or two made their escape and alarmed the town. The Col [Daniel Brodhead] . . . immediately pushed on about two miles to the Next town where he made a small halt and took a great many prisoners, soon after Magor Cochran with Capt. Grays Compy. came up and ordered me to stay with the prisoners and their two Compys. to push on to the next town about one mile forward which they did and made more prisoners and killed some particularly a Negro who was their Dr. they then plundered the houses of the most valuable things and set fire to them and Returned to the middle town where I was . . . we then collected all our prisoners plundered this town and sett fire to it then marched of[f] to the main body which lay at the first town, we stayed there about 8 hours and killed some five horses and a Number of Hogs & plundered their houses and set fire to them and Marched of[f] about 4 o'clock . . ."

*Lieutenant Erkuries Beatty, b. 1759, member of Brodhead's April raid*

stances of their being so taken and injured by the whites.

They told me in council that the whites had accused these Onondaga Indians of having had some hand with the Senecas and other tribes of Indians in warring against the Americans. But the whites were very much mistaken. In fact, they injured the Onondagas—who aren't a warlike people—without cause. The Onondagas told me that the white people thought that the Onondaga Indians might be annoying the white settlements and slaying the inhabitants there. I then considered that the whites were very wrong to make prisoners of these Indians, while they were innocent of the accusations laid upon them.

I returned to Fort Niagara, for the winter was just about to set in. Immediately after my arrival at Fort Niagara, we were called to a council by the British general. An appointment was made, and on the day and at the expiration of the hour set, we met with them.

The British general said to us: "I received a letter from Washington. He states in his letter that he has been defeated and has raised his flag for peace, and he will hereafter obey our father, the King of Great Britain. You will, therefore, remain here this winter and enjoy yourselves

Seneca sap basket or tub of elm bark

"In the fall and winter of 1779, the Six Nations of Indians whose settlements had been destroyed, went to Niagara for support and settled in poorly-constructed wigwams along the road for 8 miles above the fort, presenting the appearance of one continued Indian village from Fort Niagara to Lewiston. A great many died that winter from salt food and exposure."

*Lyman Draper, 1815–91, historian who interviewed Chainbreaker in 1850*

and eat and drink and have enough to wear and be merry for our gaining the day."

A few days afterward, four messengers arrived from Fort Stanwix. These four messengers were Indian chiefs of the Oneida. They had to come out on snowshoes, the snow was so deep, but they were so strongly desirous to make peace between the Six Nations and the Americans.

These messengers called to open a council with the Six Nations, so the Nations let the council be opened for them and allowed them to forward their object. They said in council: "We are truly sent by General George Washington that you might perfectly understand that the

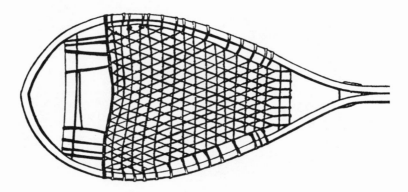

Snowshoe

war is now over and peace declared, for Great Britain is now defeated and there is no more war."

We did not believe what they said to us. How could we believe it? The

"The Senecas affirm that they can walk fifty miles per day upon the snowshoe."
*Lewis Henry Morgan*

General had just been saying that the Americans had been defeated, and now, these American messengers were saying that Great Britain had been defeated. We did not believe such a thing, and our officers took these four Oneida chiefs and imprisoned them in the Fort Niagara jail for several months. They stayed till the snow began to melt away in the spring of 1780.

About the month of March in the year 1780, the Six Nations met together to consult with each other. They concluded to have a general council with the British officers to make arrangements for the spring work, that we might plant some corn. So we met in council.

Corn husk salt bottle

"The succeeding winter [after Sullivan's Campaign] was the most severe that I have witnessed since my remembrance. The snow fell about five feet deep and remained so for a long time, and the weather was extremely cold; so much so indeed, that almost all the game upon which the Indians depended for subsistence, perished, and reduced them almost to a state of starvation. When the snow melted in the spring, deer were found dead upon the ground in vast numbers; and other animals, of every description, perished from the cold also, and were found dead in multitudes. Many of our people barely escaped with their lives, and some actually died of hunger and freezing."

*Mary Jemison*

"We now ask you, where will we sow this spring?" said Cornplanter to the British chief.

The British chief answered. He said to us to select our own location, wherever we might choose. In regard to the war, he said nothing about it, and the council was dismissed. The next day, the Six Nations of Indians met together again to select the lands where we would settle. We passed a resolution to go and settle on Buffalo Creek. That would be our own ground to rest upon and where the whole of the Six Nations would remain. So we began to make preparations to go onto it. So started, every family had their own choice of home when we came to Buffalo Creek.

About the month of April, several of us went back to Fort Niagara to get lots of hoes to work the land with and plant corn. We broke up the sod with hoes; we had no plows or cattle or work horses, so we had to do the best we could about planting things. We obtained the hoes, which the British government furnished us, and some money and hunting utensils were also furnished us at that time. At the same time, the four Oneida Indians who were in jail were discharged and returned back home without us giving them any answer to what they had brought in council.

"... we planted, tended and harvested our corn, and generally had all our children with us; but had no master to oversee or drive us, so that we could work as leisurely as we pleased."
*Mary Jemison*

Popcorn sieve

This 1771 map, which illustrates the great extent of Six Nations' territory on the eve of the Revolutionary War, also indicates the location of Chainbreaker's hometown, Canawagus. Manuscripts and Special Collections, New York State Library.

Kienrna Ba

This Country belongs
to the Oneidas

Crown Pt

Tienderoga

The Boundary of New York
not being Closed this part
of the Country still belongs
to the Mohocks

Ft Brewerton

Oneida Lk

Fish Cr

3 Rivers

DAGAS

Onondaga

Annghsaraga
Tuscarora Town

ONEIDAS

Oneida

Woods Cr

Fish Cr

Canada Cr

German Flatts

Oswego Arabia

Ft Johnson

Johnson hall

Hunter

Mohock Rr

Ft George

Ft Edward

Battenkill

Saratoga

Sacandaga

Serehtrooke

Half Moon

Bosick

TIONS

The Villages on the East Branch of
Susquehannah are chiefly occupied
by Oneidas and Tuscaroras

NEW

CherryValley

Schoharee

Batavia

Shenectady

Cohoes

Albany

YORK

Kinderhook

Claverac

Livingston

Part
of
Massachus
sets Bay

Owegy

Otsiningo

Branch of Susquehanna

Mohock Branch

Popachton Branch

Onoghquagy

Chughnut

Delaware

Katts Kill Montain

Kingston

Rhinbeck

Part
of
Connecticut

Watoosin

Pensylvania

Machapendawe Cr

Great
Swamp

PLANATION

Villages

Towns or Large Villages

Paths

dary Settled with the
768 is described by
line

Miles

To His Excellency
WILLIAM TRYON ESQr.
Captain General & Governor in Chief
of the Province of NEW-YORK & &
This Map
of the Country of the VI. Nations
Proper, with Part of the Adjacent Colonies
Is humbly inscribed by his Excellency's
Most Obedient humble Servant
Guy Johnson 1771.

113

Oil portrait of Chainbreaker c. 1845. Courtesy Rochester Museum and Science Center, Rochester, New York.

*"The Young Sachem" A Chief of the Six Nations*, painted by John Trumbull in Philadelphia in 1792. Chainbreaker may have been the sitter for this oil miniature. Courtesy Yale University Art Gallery, Trumbull Collection.

A 1796 oil portrait of Cornplanter by F. Bartoli, clearly showing the silver gorget which injured the sachem's face in the course of the carriage accident described by Chainbreaker. Collection of the New-York Historical Society, accession number 1867.314, negative number 6338.

Hand-colored engraving of an Iroquois warrior from J. Grasset de Saint
Saveur's *Encyclopedie des voyages* (1796). Courtesy National Archives of
Canada, C-003165.

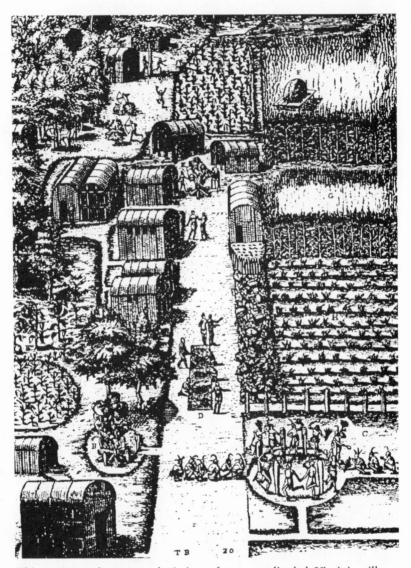

This seventeenth-century depiction of a non-palisaded Virginia village, Secotan, offers clues to the layout and appearance of Canawagus in the 1770s. Reproduced in Lewis Henry Morgan, "Houses and house-life of the American aborigines," *Contributions to American Ethnology*, Vol 4 (Washington, DC: Government Printing Office, 1881).

George Heriot's hand-colored engraving, *Costume of Domiciliated Indians of North America*, created in the first years of the nineteenth century, also provides an accurate view of Revolutionary War-era Seneca dress. Courtesy National Archives of Canada, C-012781.

Nineteenth-century engraving of British General John Burgoyne addressing Indian allies in 1777. Courtesy Fort Ticonderoga Museum.

The site of the Battle of Oriskany as it appeared in 1848. Benson J. Lossing, *Pictorial Fieldbook of the Revolution*. Vol 1 (New York: Harper & Bros, 1860).

Engraving of Joseph Brant. Benson J. Lossing, *Pictorial Fieldbook of the Revolution.*

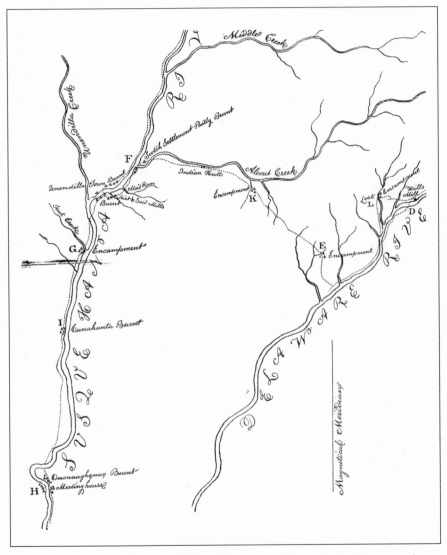

Map sketched by Captain William Gray, a participant in the Continental armies' attacks on Six Nations' villages in 1779. Frederick Cook, ed. *Journals of the Military Expedition of Major-General John Sullivan Against the Six Nations of Indians in 1779 with Records of Centennial Celebrations* (Auburn, NY: Knapp, Peck & Thomson, 1887).

Detail from a nineteenth-century engraving of Indian warriors during the Revolutionary War. Courtesy Fort Ticonderoga Museum.

Nineteenth-century engraving of imagined Revolutionary War scene with fierce warriors and cowed captives. Manuscripts and Special Collections, New York State Library.

Nineteenth-century engraving of a purely imagined and non-historical scene: Lieutenant William Boyd brought before loyalist Colonel John Butler. Manuscripts and Special Collections, New York State Library.

Nineteenth-century engraving of Major General John Sullivan, leader of the cruelly successful expedition of 1779. Manuscripts and Special Collections, New York State Library.

"Americans burning an Indian village." In John Grafton, *The American Revolution—A Picture Sourcebook* (New York: Dover Publications, 1975).

This detail from William Birch's hand-colored engraving of 1800, *Back of the State House, Philadelphia*, depicts a small group of Indians in the foreground. Was Birch attempting to memorialize one of the visits of Six Nations' dignitaries described by Chainbreaker? Courtesy The Library Company of Philadelphia.

George Washington's appearance in the 1790s. *The American Revolution—A Picture Sourcebook.*

Hand-colored engraving of Red Jacket as he appeared in the early nineteenth century. He wears the enormous silver medal presented to him by Washington in 1792. Manuscripts and Special Collections, New York State Library.

Early-twentieth-century photograph of Seneca women harvesting corn. Photograph by A.C. Parker. Courtesy W. N. Fenton.

Early-twentieth-century photograph of Seneca women husking and braiding corn. Photograph by A.C. Parker. Courtesy W. N. Fenton.

## CHAPTER SEVEN

# "Remember Me Who Rescued You"

T
he American campaigns of 1779 hurt Iroquois families more than they did warriors. Seneca war parties continued to burn frontier homes and take prisoners, though as Joseph Brant had complained in July of 1779, "The reason that we could not take more of them was owing to the many forts . . . into to which they were always ready to run like ground-hogs." In both August and October of 1780, Seneca warriors also joined British and loyalists under Sir John Johnson, old Sir William's heir, in large-scale raids on the Schoharie and Mohawk valleys in central New York. But during this time of continuing hostility, one Seneca chief extended the hand of friendship to a lone prisoner . . .

During the Revolutionary War in the year 1779 or 1780, I accompanied Cornplanter and Captain Strong, Captain Hudson, and several other warriors as they canoed downstream on the Allegheny River in the State of Pennsylvania. As we canoed between Mahoning and Kittanning, we saw smoke out amongst the trees of the heavy forest and landed on shore, and left the bark canoes, and went up on top of the riverbank. We saw quite a large company of Delaware Indians, and judging from our experience, the Delawares were making preparations to burn a prisoner at the stake.

The Delawares came out to where we Senecas stood and wanted to know if any of the Senecas could understand their language. And it happened that Captain John Hudson could understand three different languages. Along with his own, he could speak Delaware and the English language. So this enabled him to communicate with them. First, he wanted them to go and "adjourn" their burning of the white prisoner. The Delaware, not any of them, could understand the English language, and this Hudson, he went to

". . . we passed a Shawanee town, where I saw a number of heads, arms, legs, and other fragments of the bodies of some white people who had just been burnt. The parts that remained were hanging on a pole which was supported at each end by a crotch stuck into the ground, and were roasted or burnt black as coal . . ."

*Mary Jemison, from her account of a 1758 journey*

the prisoner and asked him whether he wished to be delivered from this cruel death.

"Yes, if possible," said the prisoner.

So Captain John Hudson talked with the Delawares and used his influence to let the prisoner go, and he used good reasons for this. He laid the rules before them, and Captain Hudson knew all those things, being one of the chiefs of the Seneca Nation with influence over his people and other nations.

The Delawares consulted amongst themselves and concluded to let Captain Hudson have the prisoner. The man was dealt with very kindly and untied from the post

### NOUNS OF TWO SYLLABLES.

| | | | |
|---|---|---|---|
| An-da', | Day. | Gä-ee', | Tree. |
| So-a', | Night. | Hä-ace', | Panther. |
| Gä-o', | Wind. | Je-yeh', | Dog. |
| Gus-no', | Bark. | Gen-joh', | Fish. |

### NOUNS OF THREE SYLLABLES.

| | | | |
|---|---|---|---|
| Ah-wä'-o, | Rose. | O-o'-zä, | Bass-wood. |
| O-gis'-tä, | Fire. | O-äne'-dä, | Shrub. |
| O-we'-zä, | Ice. | O-nä'-tä, | Leaf. |
| O-dus'-hote, | A spring. | Gä-ha'-neh, | Summer. |
| Gä-hä'-dä, | Forest. | O-gäs'-ah, | Evening. |
| O-eke'-tä, | Thistle. | Gä-o'-wo, | Canoe. |

### NOUNS OF FOUR SYLLABLES.

| | | | |
|---|---|---|---|
| O-na-gä'-nose, | Water. | Ong-wa-o'-weh, | Indian. |
| Gä-a-nun'-da, | Mountain. | Gä-gä-neäs'-heh, | Knife. |
| Gä-gwe-dake'-neh, | Spring. | O-gwen-nis'-hä, | Copper. |
| Sä-da'-che'-ah, | Morning. | Ah-tä-gwen'-dä, | Flint. |
| Gä-a-o'-dä, | Gun. | | |

### NOUNS OF FIVE SYLLABLES.

| | | | |
|---|---|---|---|
| Sä-da'-wä-sun-teh, | Midnight. | So-a'-kä-gä-gwä, | Moon. |
| O-wis'-tä-no-o, | Silver. | Gä-ne-o'-us-heh, | Iron. |
| An-da'-kä-gä-gwä, | Sun. | O-dä'-wä-an-do, | Otter. |

Seneca language sample

and unbound and set free to accompany Captain Hudson. Hudson told the prisoner to come along with him, for he would be saved and delivered to his friends, if the prisoner knew where his friends were. Thus Hudson rescued the white man from the stake and being burned to death.

The company started on downstream with the prisoner. As soon as we had passed out of sight of the Delaware camp, we stopped to make arrangements to escape from these Delawares, for fear they might rise up as enemies against us for taking away their prisoner. This prisoner told Hudson that his friends lived on the road leading from Pittsburgh to Philadelphia.

"About three days travel from Pittsburgh," said the prisoner.

Hudson then told the prisoner that he must go along

Another account of kind Captain Hudson:

"John Huston [Hudson] whose station was that of an Indian Chief, seems early to have taken a particular fancy to her, for, on the second night of her captivity, he spread his bearskin over her to protect her from the damp air of the night; and through all their journey to the Indian settlements at Niagara, he gave particular attention to her accomodations ... While Elizabeth remained in John Huston's family, he manifested much kindness towards her, as if he really felt a parental affection for her. He had a small kettle that he kept for his own particular use; and when he had meat, soup or hommony boiled in it, he would call Betsy to him to partake of it ..."

*Narrative of Elizabeth Gilbert; Elizabeth Gilbert, b. 1768, was taken captive by the Seneca in Pennsylvania, April 1780.*

with him, and he, Hudson, would take as straight a course as he could to strike near where the prisoner's friends lived. The prisoner replied that he would be very glad to make it home once more and see his friends.

Captain Hudson turned round to his comrades and said to them, "Go on your way toward home. Start before day and go upon the land. Don't let the Delaware Indians see you as you're going up the river, for fear they may become our enemies. We must avoid them if we possibly can. I will go with this prisoner and deliver him to his friends, and will return as soon as I can go there and come back again to our own country." This happened at the place called by the Seneca, Hr De Ga.

Cornplanter then said to the company, "We now go from here. About the time when we think a cock would crow, then we will start, and I will lead you the direct way back toward home. If we see any persons on our way that would hurt us, we will try to subdue them. But we will go home as soon as we can conveniently."

The next morning about the time a cock crows, we arose and put across the river with bark canoes. We reached the east shore of the river and disembarked and shoved our canoes into the middle of the river, letting them go downstream. And Captain Hudson bid us farewell and performed some of our own ways of ceremony on parting from friends, then put off with the prisoner behind him, to a great rejoicing.

Captain Hudson had three pieces of dry venison, each one about as big as a goose egg. But he calculated to get some more provision as they went along. The first day, they found nothing in their way to benefit or keep them. The night overtook them, and they lay out without fire,

| NAMES. | SENECA DIALECT. | SIGNIFICATION. |
|---|---|---|
| Albany. | Skä-neh'-tä-de. | Beyond the Openings. |
| Utica. | Nun-da-dä'-sis. | Around the Hill. |
| Auburn. | Dwas-co'. | A Floating Bridge. |
| Geneva. | Gä-nun-dä-sa'-ga. | A New Settlement Village. |
| Canandaigua. | Gä-nun-dä'-gwa. | A Place selected for a Settle- |
| Rochester. | Gä-sko'-sä-go. | Under the Falls.      [ment. |
| Tonawanda. | Tä'-nä-wun-da. | Swift Water. |
| Buffalo. | Do-sho'-weh. | Splitting the Fork. |
| Niagara River. | Ne-ah'-gä. | At the Neck.   (Supposed.) |
| Honeoye Lake. | Hä-ne-ä'-yeh. | A Finger Lying. |
| Hemlock Lake. | O-neh'-dä. | A Hemlock. |
| Skaneateles Lake. | Skä'-ne-o'-dice. | Long Lake. |
| Chautauque Lake. | Chä-dä'-gweh. | Place where one was lost. |
| Waterloo. | Sä'-yase. | Place of Whortleberries. |
| Herkimer. | Dä-yä-o'-geh. | At the Forks. |
| Conhocton River. | Gä-hä'-to. | A Log in the Water. |
| Oriskany Creek. | O-his'-heh. | Place of Nettles. |
| Oswego. | Swa-geh'. | Flowing out. |
| Canajoharie. | Cä-na'-jo-hä. | Washing the Basin. |
| Montezuma | Te-kä'-jik-ha'-do. | Place of Salt. |
| Schenectady. | Ho-no'-ä-go-neh'. | Pained in the Head. |
| Black River. | Gä-hun'-go-wä. | Great River. |
| Oneida Castle. | Gä-no'-ä-o-hä. | Head on a Pole. |
| Allegany River. | O-hee'-yo. | The Beautiful River. |

some ways under a tree; they lay very comfortably till daybreak. They arose and went on their course without anything to eat that morning.

It happened that about noon, or sometime in the afternoon, they came across several tribes of Indians preparing to camp or retire for the afternoon. It happened as they came to

". . . white corn was roasted brown and pounded slowly in a mortar and sifted until all the granules were uniform . . . Preserved in skin bags, this meal was carried by hunters and either eaten raw with water, boiled . . . or thrown in with boiling meat."
*Arthur C. Parker*

the nearest one, Hudson began to talk with them. He found they were of the same tribe that he was himself—and the rest of the companies, they were of some other tribe. Each tribe had built one very good fire at some length from those of the others. Captain Hudson and his partner [*once prisoner!*] ate with them. They ate the dried venison—the same article they had when they started from the river.

They stayed with these Indians all afternoon and part of the night. That evening, Captain Hudson heard some conversation amongst the other tribes concerning the prisoner. According to the appearance of things, a controversy about him was increasing, so that Hudson was afraid they might try to take his prisoner away from him. He made up his mind to escape from them and get out of their reach. Mr. Hudson told his companion what the Indians had said about him and about Hudson's fears that they might take the prisoner and Hudson, himself, too. Hudson told him that they must put out at the first opportunity, as soon as it became dark in the evening. Hudson told the Indians that he had to go visit at another Indian fire about twenty rods distant. He pretended that he would come back and stay with them during the night.

They let him go, and both men went about halfway between the two fires, where Hudson told his friend to go

## Varieties of Iroquois beans

*Beans, osai''dă'*

| | |
|---|---|
| Bush beans | dega'gahă' |
| Wampum | o'tgo'ä osai''dă' |
| Purple kidney | awe'oñdago$^n$ |
| White kidney | o'sai''dăgän |
| Marrowfat | osai''dowanĕs |
| String | { otgo$^n$'wasäga$^n$oñ<br>{ odji'stanokwa |
| Cornstalk | oä''geka |
| Cranberry | hayuk'osai''dăt |
| Chestnut lima | onii'stă' |
| Hummingbird | djŭtowĕndo$^n$ |
| White (small) | osai''dagä'n |
| Wild peas | owĕndo'ge'ă' osai''dă' |
| Bean vines | oo$^n$'să' |
| Poles | yoäno'dă'kwă' |

to a place which he described. He must stay there very still till Captain Hudson came. So they parted; the prisoner went according to the direction and stopped, and Mr. Hudson went to the camp. He told them he had merely come to see them, to see how they were getting along. He told them that he wanted to go on to the next fire and see how they were getting along there and learn of their plans ["prospect their objects"].

He stayed a few moments, and then went on to where his friend was, and they went on toward another fire. Captain Hudson managed the same as he did at the first fire. So they went past two fires. Mr. Hudson then said to his companion that they must try to leave the Indian companies, for it felt unsafe to be with them any longer.

So they put out in a certain direction in the darkest time of the night. Mr. Hudson guided his course by the stars—although it was partly cloudy that night—and they traveled all night long for fear that they would be taken by those Indians. However, they escaped from the danger which appeared to threaten them, according to the conversation they had heard.

They traveled on till noon. They came across a small deer, shot and killed it. Captain Hudson took the whole deer on his back and carried it to a hidden place or gulf where they stopped and built a fire and roasted the deer. They stayed there all the afternoon. Just at night, they started on, about half a mile, and then stopped to retire for the night, lying down by the side of a tree without fire. In the middle of the night, rain descended and put them to trouble sleeping. They had to bear this suffering caused by the rain and want of sleep till daylight, when they started on their course till the night of the third day.

On the fourth day of their journey, in the afternoon, they came to where cattle tracks appeared. This satisfied them that inhabitants couldn't be a great way off. They approached on their direct course till they came to improvements [*cleared land*] and the

"In the fall [of 1780], John Huston [Hudson], the head of the family, went out on a hunting expedition; and as he was returning, he took a heavy cold from his careless manner of lying in the wet; and thereby lost the use of his limbs for a long time."

*Account of Abner Gilbert's Captivity; Abner, b. 1763, was the brother of Elizabeth Gilbert.*

young man grew cheerful and glad at the prospect of see-ing his friends.

Captain Hudson then ordered a stop in plain sight of the cabin. He said to his friend, or to the prisoner, "Give me your hand!" The young man gave it, and Hudson took his hand and said to him, "You will now go away and see your friends. Remember me who rescued you from the hands of those who passed upon you a sentence of death by fire, the work of the hands of the Delaware Nation. Remember not only me, but all the Seneca Nation, for I am a Seneca chief. I therefore say to you to remember my nation and fight no more against me."

And they parted. The young man went one way, and Captain Hudson went the other and passed on. This prisoner, I don't know his name, although his children are now residing about sixty or seventy miles from Pittsburgh in a stone house on the left-hand side of the road coming from Pittsburgh. The family was a wealthy family, Hudson supposed.

## CHAPTER EIGHT

# "We Won't Give Up Our Lands"

O ne year after the new United States signed a peace
treaty with Great Britain, United States officials
forced a peace tied to major—almost total—land
concessions from the Iroquois. Though Chainbreaker and other
Iroquois always maintained that they never ratified or fully
accepted the 1784 Treaty of Fort Stanwix, the United States
government "kept it on the books." And later treaties only
modified it slightly.

Some newly-liberated colonials consciously worked to
break down Iroquois pride and identity at Fort Stanwix. On
the eve of the council, New York landowner and politico James
Duane wrote to one negotiator: "I would never suffer the word
'Nation' or 'Six Nations,' or 'Confederates,' or 'Council Fire at
Onondago' or any other form which would revive or seem to
confirm their former ideas of independence, to escape . . . they

*are used to be called Brethren, Sachems & Warriors of the Six Nations. I hope it will never be repeated."*

About the month of August in the year 1784, Washington sent a delegation to us for the purpose of making a treaty—one white man and one Oneida chief on the part of the United States. They notified us that Washington wished us to hold a council with him at Fort Stanwix. We considered whether the Six Nations would agree to go or not; there was some controversy amongst us. But three chiefs were willing and in favor of going: Cornplanter, Brant, Red Jacket. I, myself, and others of the different tribes were also willing to go as delegates to Fort Stanwix; forty Indians in all were ready to go. Thus, an appointment was made for a day to start. It took us seven days to reach there.

Two days after we arrived, the council opened with the Oneidas prepared for peace. But we gave no answer at this time. At eight o'clock in the morning of the first day, the American officer rose in council and said, "I was sent by General Washington to open the council with you, all the Six Nations of Indians, as brothers and to make peace, and let you know that we have defeated Great Britain and settled with them. The British have given up their claim to a certain portion of this continent, and the people who fought for them have signed over their titles to us.

"We call you to council to make a treaty with you, for we do not wish to set ourselves and you to annoying each

"There was a treaty at Tioga Point—the year I don't recollect—between the agents of the government and the Indian tribes. The most of the Indians who assembled then came upon the headwaters of this river. I saw them coming down in their canoes—saw them first at the bend of the river above the village. There were several hundred canoes—some four to six Indians in a canoe—a good many squaws and young Indians among them. The canoes were of bark. It was a handsome sight as they approached the village. They came in such fine order. They came in a solid body and with great regularity and uniform movement—some of them ornamented with feathers, some with jewels. Covered with brooches, generally of silver. Generally with white woolen blankets with heavy stripes. Some had head-cloths of blankets. The Indian men were generally of pretty good stature. They had their rifles, tomahawks and scalping knives with them, pipes and their kind of tobacco. They commenced landing at or near my father's house and so along down as far as McMark's house. Between the two houses was a plain beautiful and green. They were very good-natured; they were then all for peace. Their diversion was to cut and repair their ornaments—worked into their garments with porcupine quills and painted on. Leggings, breech cloths, blankets, headdress, moccasins, and ornaments were their costume."

*Jesse McQuigg*

other any longer. Great Britain has no more to do with you, for we have divided all the lands and lakes from east to west, from ocean to ocean: one half of Lake Ontario and Lake Erie, and so on across Lake Superior, direct to the ocean. We have exchanged receipts and written con-

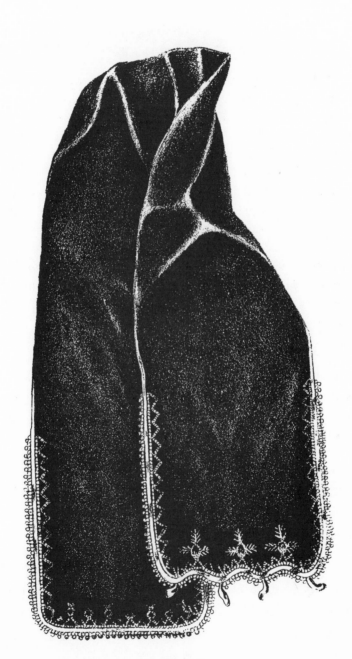

Breech cloth

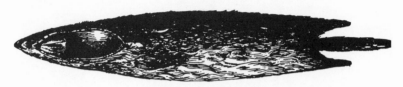

Tobacco pouch

tracts with the British. We also have a letter for you [*swearing*] to these facts."

So he handed over this letter to Brant. Brant took it in his hand and read a few lines and began to swear and stamp down, and he turned his face right round toward us and said, "We have been deceived by the King of Great Britain. Therefore, we will not stay here another minute. We will go back, and we won't give up our lands as the British did."

So we left the ground and went back to our camps. There we held private council by ourselves to exhort each other on the best course to pursue. Brant offered his resolution; that was, to continue fighting for his right, for he

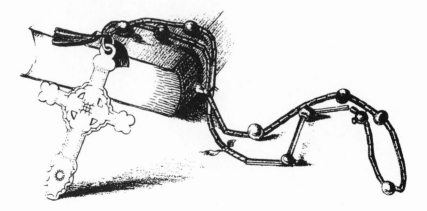

Necklace

144

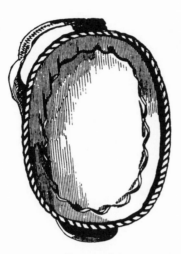

Silver medal

was willing to die for his right and his country in the struggle with America. Cornplanter was not satisfied with the language which the Americans had used in council. He wanted to understand more and talk with them more concerning this. Red Jacket wanted to go and see Washington. I, myself, had the same wish: to understand more on the subject and to hear the proposition again from Washington, because I had been in communication with Washington before, and I knew well his feelings about making a treaty with us.

We continued in controversy all the afternoon and all night. The warriors said noth-

"He was tall and rather thin. His look was fierce and frightful. His apparel was becoming and rich, a broadcloth blanket with a rich border, and otherwise elegantly dressed. He looked splendid to my childish eyes with his shining epaulettes and superb appearance."

*Jane Strope Whitaker, on seeing Joseph Brant at Fort Niagara before the war's end*

145

"She was dressed in a short skirt reaching a little below her knees—made of imported blue cloth and beautifully-worked pantalettes of blue cloth and other material to meet the skirt. The skirt was ornamented with brooches as were the clothes of the warriors. They all had small bells on their moccasin strings and pantalettes. They used the blankets, varying them [varying the tying] as did the males.

"The squaws did not paint their faces. They never appeared disposed to harm us."

*Jane Strope Whitaker*

ing; they just listened. Some of the Oneida young women stayed with us that night—with those who favored the American side—and they learned of the controversy and Brant's resolution. Finally, toward morning, Brant called the rest of the chiefs "cowards" in order to encourage them to go on. These Oneida young women rose about daybreak and went back to their camps and told their chiefs what had been said during the night about the warfare.

The Oneida chiefs came over to see Brant to make him understand the proposition which Washington had made to the Six Nations of Indians. That was to let the Six Nations live, and give them a certain proportion of land to live on and be at peace, if only they would hear Washington's advice. The Oneida advised the Six Nations to take the offer.

Brant then cooled off his ambitions, and he said, "I will now grant [*accept*] all this along with you, and I will depart and go to the King of Great Britain and make him good for all the deceiving he has done us. And you, Cornplanter and Red Jacket and others, go and see

Washington and transact [*this business*] with Washington. Don't let him cheat you or deceive you in making a treaty, and I will do what I can with the King." So Brant left us on this ground on the same day.

On the next, we were called to council, and the American told the Six Nations that Washington had sent him to treat with the Indian brothers, and he therefore came and saw them with good will. He said, "I will now present [*this matter*] as Washington would do with you, word for word: 'If you stop annoying me, I will give you land that is good.'"

Cornplanter rose up and said, "We ask nothing about having land, for we have lands without you. But we will hear you." Said Cornplanter also, "You will always be annoying my Indians."

"I will not do anything if you agree with me to stop it, and stop setting our people to fighting," said the white man to the Indians. "I therefore now request you to live and be at peace and be a distinct and independent nation. You will have a tract of land sufficient to make a residence for all the Six Nations. I will give you the description of this particular place: the boundary begins about one mile below Fort Niagara from the first creek which comes out of the lake, beginning just north of the creek and run-

"The soil of the earth from one end of the land to the other is the property of the people who inhabit it. By birthright the Ongwehonweh (Original beings) are the owners of the soil which they own and occupy and none other may hold it."

*The Constitution of the Five Nations*

ning along the lake shore up to the mouth of the Niagara River, and running up the river along the south bank of the river, and taking in Grant Island. So it runs up to eight miles below the mouth of Buffalo Creek 'to the corner,' and thence southward to the Allegheny River about two miles below the mouth of Olean Creek or Point. It crosses the river to a point five or six miles south of the river 'to the corner,' and thence northeastward, taking in the Genesee River and coming out near Oneida, on the north side of it. There, is made another 'corner,' and thence to the place mentioned at the beginning." This was the description he made to us in council.

We did not accept the offer the first day, not until four or five days afterward. Before Cornplanter gave his consent, the rest of the chiefs had to consent and take the deed to the tract of land which the white man offered for our settlement in this time of difficulty. The question ["controversy"] was decided upon condition, that is, on leaving, we would take that deed with us to our people to say whether they would accept and receive the offer or

Seashell medal

not. The white man had to agree to this. Thus, the council was dismissed, and we came home to Buffalo Creek in the month of October 1784.

After we had rested, our peacemakers called to open the general council, our people's assembly, to explain to them what was transacted at the Fort Stanwix council and what offer was made by General Washington to the Six Nations. So we notified them in all quarters, and all came to the council. So met in council Cornplanter, Red Jacket, and Young King, and several of the other peacemakers of the different nations of Indians. Cornplanter and Red Jacket took the stand and gave the blessing—which they always do before speaking on any great and important subject—that Our Maker guard and save our homes.

At the end of the ceremony, they gave an account of the language which had been used at the Fort Stanwix council, and all the transactions between the two parties, Washington and the Six Nations, and an explanation of their deeds.

At this very time, Joseph Brant returned home from England. Brant asked the people to allow him to take the load off his back before we took the load off ours. So the warriors let him go on and tell us what he had done with Great Britain.

"... in opening the council [the sachem] shall hold the strands of shells in his hands when speaking. When he finishes speaking he shall deposit the strings on an elevated place (or pole) so that all the assembled Lords [sachems] and the people may see it and know that the council is open and in progress."

*The Constitution of the Five Nations*

The Pigeon Grounds

" . . . a runner came in shouting Yu-ak-oo-was! Yu-ak-oo-was! (Pigeons! Pigeons!) He said the birds had roosted in a wood on the Genesee River about two days journey above Caneadea Village. All was now bustle and confusion and every person in the village who could bear the fatigue of travel at once set out for the Genesee. On their arrival at the place . . . Jones beheld a sight that he never forgot . . . Each tree and branch bore nests on every available spot. The birds had exhausted every species of nesting material in the vicinity including small twigs of the trees and the ground was as bare as though swept with a broom. The eggs were hatching and thousands of squabs filled the nests . . . As the annual nesting of the pigeons was a matter of great importance to the Indians who depended largely upon the supply of food thus obtained, runners carried the news to every part of the Seneca territory and the inhabitants singly and in bands came from as far east as Seneca Lake and as far north as Lake Ontario . . . Fires were made in front of the cabins and bunches of the dressed birds were suspended on poles sustained by crotched sticks. When properly cured they were packed in bags and baskets for transportation to the home towns."

**Life of Horatio Jones**

Joseph Brant said, "I have reserved land in Canada sufficient to keep all the Thirteen Nations [*the Six Nations of the Iroquois Confederacy—Seneca, Onondaga, Mohawk, Cayuga, Oneida, and Tuscarora—plus seven other Iroquoian peoples, probably the Wyandot, Potawatomi, Chippewa, Shawnee, Kickapoo, Delaware, and Miami*]. Its situation commences at the mouth of the

Grand River. It is twelve miles wide and as long as the head of the river. It would be sufficient for all the different Indian nations, for their residence and hunting grounds and fishing rivers and creeks, and all water privileges and trapping privileges in the ponds.

"And three hundred thousand in gold money has already been paid over to us, and a large quantity of goods are to be provided for us by Great Britain annually. The annuity is to be paid by an agent appointed by the British government, payable at Fort Niagara, and no duty to be paid on our goods crossing over the Niagara River to our side."

All these offers were accepted by our people, and they signed onto the stipulations of the British treaty with the Thirteen Nations of Indians residing in Canada and in the eastern United States. On the part of the Indians, all was then satisfied and agreed to concerning the British treaty with the Thirteen Nations of Indians. So the council was closed and adjourned till the next day.

Joseph Brant then rather wanted the Six Nations to go over to Canada to make a permanent home together with all the Indian nations to establish their own customs and traditions—the different tribes of Indians—and their own regulations, and to live once more as an independent government. The Six Nations rather refused to do so. When the next day the question was raised about removal to Canada, they called on the wisest of the middle-aged women to see what they said on the subject of removal to Canada to make a permanent home there forever. It was left to them whether we would go or not.

The women decided that the Six Nations would remain on the south side of the line between America and Great Britain—for, in future, the Canadians might be obliged to remove or might be driven off their lands. Then, the Canadians might have to share with us, and if we should be driven off or deprived of our lands, we would have to share with them. In justice, we would have to accept whatever was given to us—an impossible situation.

We took the women's advice, together with our own, and decided not to go to Canada at present. This was decided in council at Black Rock on the third day from the commencement of the council. The council then adjourned till the next, or fourth day, when Brant asked the Six Nations whether they [*each nation and each warrior*] wanted to have the right to take their choice of the two countries—that is, with some for Canada and some for staying in the States. Brant wished to have a part of all the nations go to Canada, though some would remain here. The Mohawk chief then arose and said, "My people

Squash shell rattles

will go to Canada with King Brant." Brant was a Mohawk himself, so of course his people would go with him wherever he went.

The Cayugas were divided. Some went back to Utica—about four families; some remained amongst the Senecas at Buffalo; some went with Brant over to Canada; and some went up the lake to Sandusky and settled there. The Tuscaroras were also divided. Some went over to Canada; some remained on our side of the boundary, settled near Lewiston, about seven miles below Niagara Falls, where they made a permanent home to establish their own customs of their nation. The Senecas were also divided in this way. Some went over to Canada with Joseph Brant, and some went up the lake to Sandusky and there settled their permanent home to enjoy their own privileges and the custom of their own councils and worship.

"Six regular festivals, or thanksgivings, were observed by the Iroquois. The first, in order of time, was the Maple festival. This was a return of thanks to the maple itself, for yielding its sweet waters. Next was the Planting festival, designed chiefly, as an invocation of the Great Spirit to bless the seed. Third came the Strawberry festival, instituted as a thanksgiving for the first fruits of the earth. The fourth was the Green Corn festival, designed as a thanksgiving acknowledgment for the ripening of corn, beans, and squashes. Next was celebrated the Harvest festival, instituted as a general thanksgiving to "Our Supporters," after the gathering of the harvest. Last in the enumeration is placed the New Year's festival, the great jubilee of the Iroquois, at which the White Dog was sacrificed."

*Lewis Henry Morgan*

"The Senecas have a . . . legend that they sprang from the ground at Nun-da-wa-o [at the head of Lake Canandaigua]."
*Lewis Henry Morgan*

. A large number of families remained at Buffalo, in Cattaraugus County, and on the Allegheny and Genesee Rivers. Several thousand souls of the Seneca remained in the State of New York. The Oneidas, they went back to their old homestead, but a few went over to Canada. The Onondagas remained where they now live, to enjoy their own privileges on their own land. Thus, all the nations have separated in all directions, with their residences in different countries. The Senecas are the head nation of all Six Nations of Indians residing in the State of New York.

The council then consulted amongst themselves on the subject of Washington's proposal. It was all written down on a piece of skin. It took them two days before they fairly understood all of it. They came to the conclusion that they would not take or receive the deed and offer made by General Washington, and they passed resolutions to continue the war. They weren't willing to give up their rights to the soil, which they considered actually belonged to them. They did not believe that Washington,

Snow-snake

or any other white man, had any right to deed us any lands while at the same time the land belonged to the Indians.

We, therefore, were willing to suffer the consequences [*of this decision*] unless Washington would give us a better offer than he had heretofore. We would then take another consideration, if this was the case. So delegations were appointed; Red Jacket, Cornplanter, and myself, Chainbreaker, were proper delegates, and also Young King and several other chiefs of the Six Nations. The delegations were appointed to take this deed of land back to Washington, and for us to tell Washington of the resolution passed in our council in the month of October 1784. That was the resolution to continue the war.

We made preparation to start before the snow fell that fall. Several families started with us. We went along the lake shore as far as the small settlement called Erie, and from there, south, and so

"Gawasa or Snow-snake . . . Among the amusements of the winter season, in Indian life, was the game with Snow-snakes . . . The snake was thrown with the hand by placing the forefinger against its foot, and supporting it with the thumb and remaining fingers. It was thus made to run upon the snow crust with the speed of an arrow, and to a much greater distance, sometimes running sixty or eighty rods . . . The snakes were made of hickory, and with the most perfect precision and finish. They were from five to seven feet in length, about a fourth of an inch in thickness, and gradually diminishing from about an inch in width at the head, to about half an inch at the foot. The head was round, turned up slightly, and pointed with lead to increase the momentum of the snake."

*Lewis Henry Morgan*

entered the stream of French Creek, and on to what is now Midville, and so on down to the mouth of French Creek. We made a stop with the few white families living at the mouth, for they were acquaintances of some of the Indians. They were good people and visited amongst the Indians as well as amongst their own kind of folks while we were there building our bark canoes to proceed down the river with. We were soon ready to go down and went about seven miles to Big Sandy Creek. We stayed there over the winter with several Indian families. We were neighbors to each other while camping for winter hunting, enjoying and supporting ourselves this way throughout the winter.

CHAPTER NINE

# "The War Was Now Closed"

I n 1786, an Iroquois delegation traveled to Pittsburgh,
Philadelphia, and New York City, as Chainbreaker relates.
But, contrary to Chainbreaker's account, the Iroquois met
with George Washington in the course of another trip in 1790,
and this meeting took place in Philadelphia, not New York
City.

By late 1790, the federal capital had moved to the
Pennsylvania city, then the largest and wealthiest in the nation.
The presence of the national government supplied new excitement and glamor to already glamorous Philadelphia. A
Republican court formed around Washington and attracted fine
artists like Benjamin West and Jonathan Trumbull. Trumbull
was probably the one who painted Chainbreaker's portrait
under the title, "The Young Sachem, a Chief of the Six
Nations." The painting, which survives in the Yale University

*Art Gallery, bears the date, 1792, so it's possible memories of three different trips coalesce in the account that follows.*

Early in the spring of the year 1786, the delegations started for the meeting with Washington. We first went to Pittsburgh to see a certain man there, who well understood the Seneca and Cayuga languages, to act as our interpreter with Washington. He was a white man by the name of Joseph Dickinson. When we arrived at Pittsburgh, we made inquiries about where Joseph Dickinson was; Cornplanter wanted to see him. Joseph Dickinson soon appeared and communicated with Cornplanter regarding the warfare. He told us that one or two men had come back from down the river. They had been with an army sent down there alone and all destroyed by the western Indians of several different tribes. An officer was sent by General Washington to make a treaty and peace—to war no more. But those Indians refused and destroyed his army, and but a very few escaped. These men had just arrived in town that morning, and the officer was already on his way to see Washington concerning the business.

After we learned this, we felt distressed and were desirous to see these men. So we invited Mr. Dickinson to go with us. We saw the two men, and we communicated with them, for we had a good interpreter with us, easy for each of us to understand. This enabled one to tell us about the business, and he told us the same story Mr. Dickinson

Work bag

had been telling us. Cornplanter told him, in turn, our business: that we were now on the way to General Washington to make a treaty with all the different tribes of Indians; the Six Nations and the American people and all the Native Indians wished to have a treaty with the help of Washington.

159

An Account of Cornplanter:
"He spread them a couch of the long grass which grew near the camping place, offered them a portion of his own stock of dried meat and parched corn . . . To the day of her death, she remembered with tenderness and gratitude her brother, the Big White Man [Cornplanter] and her friends and playfellows among the Senecas."

*The Capture by the Indians of Little Eleanor Lytle*; *Lytle, b. 1771, was captured "on the banks of the Plum River" in Pennsylvania in 1779 and adopted by Cornplanter's mother.*

The white man, our interpreter, then wished us to wait for him five days. He would be one of the companions to go with us to Washington, and would be ready by that time. So we told him we would wait, and we felt glad to do so. After five days, we were ready to start all together on foot. As we went along the road on the way to Philadelphia, we found but a few inhabitants beside the road on the way. And generally, these families left their cabins as soon as they saw us coming on toward them. They had to run across lots, sometimes. The white man with us hallooed at them, for them to come back, for we weren't going to hurt them in any way. But they would run away from us. They were

Seneca stone mortar and muller

160

afraid of Indians. I suppose because we look like such a savage people with such an uncivilized appearance when we are engaged to go to war. Most every family we came to, they ran or hid themselves away from our sight for fear that we would hurt them while we were traveling during the sixty-seven days of our journey.

Mr. Dickinson, the interpreter, said to the company that he would go ahead so that the next family we came to—he would have a conversation with the family—so as not to have them run when we came, so we might exchange compliments with them, and they wouldn't be so fearful of us. Cornplanter told Dickinson that he wished he would do so, as we might also want to buy bread from them—for he thought we needed it—as well as have a better acquaintance with them.

I told the company, "I feel desirous to go with Mr. Dickinson. The family will not be afraid of me, for I am young and not a bad-looking fellow." Uncle Cornplanter told me I might go with Dickinson. So we went on forward till we came to the next house. There was nobody living in it, and we went on by till the next house.

Dickinson entered this house, and I stood nearby at the door till Dickinson called me in. I went in and saw the gentleman and his wife and children. I offered to shake hands with the gentleman, and he received me, and his wife also, but the children refused. They cried right out. I told them that I wasn't going to hurt them, but was a friend to them and wished they would feel the same toward me, for I felt friendship with them all for the war was now closed. And therefore, we ought to feel sorrow

"The weather being severe—the roads bad—and the Indians much fatigued, I thought it best to let them remain a few days, and see the place [Carlisle, Pennsylvania] The principal inhabitants of the town and country shewed them many marks of attention, which gave them great satisfaction. I then had them sent under the same gentleman's care, at the chiefs request, to Philadelphia, where I overtook them. The beauty of the country they had passed thro'—the magnitude of the city—the numbers of people, shipping & curiosities to them quite new induced the chief to request their being indulged with a few days stay, with which I complied, judging it proper that they should have just impressions of the strength, opulence and consequence of so much of the United States…"

*Richard Butler, United States Commissioner of Indian Affairs, in a letter to "the President of Congress" dated April 25, 1786*

now for what had already been done by human beings, for we were now on the way to see Washington to make a treaty with the different nations of Indians, and there would be peace for all mankind.

This family gave us all the bread they could spare, and some meat, without charging anything for what they let us have. They invited us to stay by the family overnight, and we did so. The next morning they wished us to stay for breakfast, and we agreed. The gentleman then went on to tell the story of something which had happened about three years earlier. He said twenty-five or thirty Indians had destroyed a small army about halfway from this place to Harrisburg. But a very few escaped, and he was one of them. One of his own officers was taken prisoner by the Indians and was kept amongst the Indians for about two

Pocket book

months. Then an Indian captain rescued the white man, who was a wealthy man. The Indian captain's name was Captain Hudson, and Captain Hudson took this white man and delivered him near to the white man's house.

163

Captain Hudson told the prisoner, "Go your way and remember me." So the Indian left this white man; the white man came home to his friends, who hadn't expected to ever see him again, and the man yet lived.

Then we were called to our breakfast and had to leave the conversation with the gentleman. After breakfast, we started on about three days' travel before we arrived at a small village thirty miles from Philadelphia. We stopped at the house of a gentleman who came with us from Pittsburgh. He called us to a certain room; we all went in by ourselves. After we had rested, this gentleman and his folks came into the room, and our interpreter was with them. The gentleman told us through the interpreter that he wanted us to stay with him eight or ten days at his house, for he calculated to get clothes made for us, white people's clothes—in fashion and at his own expense.

We wanted to know the reason for this. He said that it might prevent the white families being afraid of us because of being dressed Indian-style. Cornplanter, Red Jacket, Young King, and myself consented, staying till we had the clothes made up.

While we remained in this place, we had very good times with these people—hunting deer and foxes, chasing them with dogs. The people of the neighborhood grew acquainted with us, as we did with them, and we lived peaceably and happily, enjoying ourselves with them and the good living while we remained at this house. At the time our clothes were all made up, every man was suited with his own coat, the colors chosen at the time of cutting.

Needle book

We stayed at this place ten days, till we started on again with all the company. This gentleman went along with us, and Dickinson, the interpreter of the Six Nations. The inhabitants along the road, they appeared contented with us and not so fearful as they had been before when we had our other clothes on. We felt more at peace with the whites on the road between the place where we obtained the clothes and Philadelphia. It took us two days' travel to arrive in Philadelphia. There we were to stop, according to the orders from headquarters.

We had to wait ten days before we heard from Washington and learned where he was and when he would be in New York. While we stayed in this city, Cornplanter and myself were called to a certain street and house with our interpreter. So we went one morning. There we saw a gentleman who wished us to let them draw our likenesses, and they would give us other great mens' likenesses, or pay us for it, if we chose. Uncle Cornplanter consented, so, of course, I did too. So they went to work on the portraits.

At about the time our portraits were done, our company was ready to start for New York City. We went abroad in coaches or carriages and went on toward New York. While riding during the day, the coach which I was in with Cornplanter and one of the two white men capsized. The white man was hurt some by falling against his face on the ground, and he broke his spectacles and hurt his eyes a little. The Cornplanter used to wear a piece of silver metal [*a British military "gorget,"* *a mark of rank*] under his chin, or on his breast rather, which was thrown to his face and struck on his brow over the left eye and cut a considerable gash at that time. Probably some of you have taken notice of this, if you ever saw him when he was alive. His brow was lopped down; it nearly covered over his eye.

This was only some of the bad luck on the way of our journey. Our being a great deal "handed about" in our carriage—this hurt and injured it. And our determination was to get to New York that day. So our driver had to go and get another

"On friday last I set out with them for this place—but the unfortunate accident of the stage over-Setting and injuring both myself and the chief, has prevented my giving your Excellency earlier information that they arrived in this city on Sunday last. I have put them into good lodgings and the chief under the hand of a Surgeon, & I expect that in two or three days, his wound will be so well as to enable him to pay his respects to your Excellency & Congress . . ."
*Richard Butler, letter of April 25*

carriage. Therefore, we did not reach New York until the next morning after breakfast, when we crossed the river.

It was two days after our arrival in town before Washington appeared before us and made himself known to us. He wanted us to come to his office and to let him know our objects [*purpose*]. Some of his officers gave us orders to go to any grocery and provision stores and get what we wanted to eat while we stayed with him. I, for one, went after the provisions with the order, and several others went with me and obtained the things.

The next day in the morning, the chiefs and others all went to Washington's office. There I saw three officers: one stood on one side of the doorway, another on the other side, and one in the middle—all well armed with guns and swords—to guard Washington. They would not let us in for a few minutes till some other officer came to the door and invited us into the house. We all went in and saw more than one hundred and fifty men in one large room, and they gave us seats.

The Washington got up and said, "Who are you all, and who is the head chief amongst you, and what nation do you all belong to, or what tribes? How many tribes are you, and what is your business here? I wish you now to present it before this assembly of my people, and give us your object, and I will give you an answer," said the Washington.

Cornplanter rose and said, "Firstly, I am the head, and Red Jacket and I are the chief warriors and head chiefs of the Six Nations. We are of the Seneca Tribe, and with us are several other chiefs belonging to other tribes. We were appointed by our people in our General Council; these delegations are legal—the just and proper persons to deal with you.

"You have already settled the difficulty between you and Great Britain, and the British chief has given up a certain proportion of this continent from the ocean to the ocean, and half of Lake Ontario, and so on up the Niagara

Indian flute

168

River, and also on Lake Erie and Lake Huron and Lake Superior, so direct on a southwest course to the ocean. This is the description. The British King gave you everything on the south side of the above-mentioned lakes to establish your own government, and he gave you a title.

"You also have provided for us—all the Six Nations—to remain on a certain tract of land sufficient for us, and described and laid down on a piece of skin, plainly written, and together with the treaty for us to sign. Upon these grounds, there is to be no more war with you and a declaration of peace for all nations.

"But our people are not satisfied with the size of the land calculated for the Six Nations. [*All*] the land yet remains in our hands till we ratify the treaty—or whatever it is—for we have not given up yet. If Great Britain has, we care nothing about them, for they are cowards. My people will not accept the offer unless you do better. And I will say no more at present."

"I cannot give you an answer. You must remain here till I am ready to give you an answer," said the Washington.

So we remained thirty days before Washington gave us an answer on the subject. Said he, "My people have taken a deep consideration of your affairs, and they have come to the conclusion, on their best sense and determination, to let the wars be done away with and drop down under the ground—to see them no more. They, therefore, will make additions to the offer of 1784, and they have arranged the best for all of us, all the nations which have lived through the dreadful Affliction.

"It was the custom of the Genesee Indians when game was scarce to go to Lake Erie to catch a kind of fish which they called Skis-tu-wa . . . These were opened and dried in smoke, large quantities often being carried to the home towns."

*Life of Horatio Jones*

"Now we will make you a certificate of our treaty. You may have a choice and give us the description, and we will grant it according to your wishes, from beginning to end, any quantity of land, as you see sufficient for the Six Nations to remain on and be contented to live by yourselves," said the Washington.

Cornplanter then stood up and said to them, "You, the white man, come from the other side of the Big Waters where your brother, Great Britain, lives. You have fought with him to gain liberty and you have gained the day. It is right, for he is a deceiver, as he has deceived the Six Nations of Indians, those you call 'red men'. But we are true Americans. We live here on this continent. Our God created us here; the Lord gave us all these lands. I have a right to make a reserve for my people to live on, since the land belongs to the Indians. I will reserve land for my people to our satisfaction.

"I will now make the description. Commencing at the south 'corner' on the south side of the Allegheny River at the place cited in 1784, page 28, the addition is to run down from the river to the state line between New York and Pennsylvania, and follow westerly to Cannonwango Creek, and follow up the middle of the stream, which we will reserve for our fishing ground. So it runs up to Lake

The strange but true story of Cornplanter and his father:

"The next summer after Sullivan's campaign, our Indians . . . determined to obtain some redress by destroying their frontier settlements. Corn Planter, otherwise called John O'Bail, led the Indians, and an officer by the name of Johnston commanded the British in the expedition . . . when they came to Fort Plain, on the Mohawk river, Corn Planter and a party of his Indians took old John O'Bail, a white man, and made him a prisoner . . . After he had taken the old man, his father, he led him as a prisoner ten or twelve miles up the river, and then stepped before him, faced about, and addressed him in the following terms:

'My name is John O'Bail, commonly called Corn Planter. I am your son! You are my father! You are now my prisoner, and subject to the customs of Indian warfare; but you shall not be harmed; you need not fear. I am a warrior! Many are the scalps which I have taken! Many prisoners I have tortured to death! I am your son! I am a warrior! I was anxious to see you, and to greet you in friendship. I went to your cabin and took you by force! But your life shall be spared. Indians love their friends and their kindred, and treat them with kindness. If you choose to follow the fortune of your yellow son, and to live with our people, I will cherish your old age with plenty of venison, and you shall live easy: But if it is your choice to return to your fields and live with your white children, I will send a party of my trusty young men to conduct you back in safety. I respect you, my father; you have been friendly to Indians, and they are your friends.'

Old John chose to return. Corn Planter, as good as his word, ordered an escort to attend him home, which they did with the greatest care."

*Mary Jemison*

Chautauqua, and we will reserve one-half of that lake; so directly northwest to Lake Erie and thence on down along the edge of the water to the other 'corner,' eight miles from the mouth of Buffalo Creek—the same place cited in 1784 on page 28 of this book. If you grant this description made before you, we will be satisfied."

Washington then rose and said to us, "We will grant this description. You will have these lands to make a residence there and to enjoy by yourselves. And none of my people will be allowed to reside on your reservation, or attempt to deal with you, or to reside within the boundary. You will have the authority to remove them, or any men hunting, and take their goods.

"You will live by yourselves and be an independent nation and act as your own government, and I will act as my government for the good of my people. You will do the same, and there will be peace for all the nations. You will obtain this for your children and your children's children forever. Your land will remain in your hands forever, as long as the sun rises and the water runs and the grass grows on earth. This is the bargain. It is made as good as this: you may keep the lands as long as I have mentioned, but you may sell at any time that you see fit and sell any quantity of your land to your satisfaction. I will not interfere if the sale is to my people, not to foreigners."

Now Cornplanter rose and expressed his gladness for the guarantees of our lands by the United States' Washington. They then told us to stay till the contract was written and all the treaty stipulations [terms] compiled, and

Rattle made from a dried squash

the whole signed by the Six Nations and George Washington on behalf of the United States.

During the twelve days we had to stay longer, Washington used to call on us and sit together with us, telling stories and talking of the character of human nature of different nations—all what little he had learned. He was then only thirty-eight or thirty-nine years of his age, and he only told stories from his youth up until this time. [*Washington, b. 1732, was actually fifty-eight.*] Red Jacket used to be a "machine" with Washington, telling stories. Both understood the business well.

During this time, Washington made me a chief of the Six Nations and made me a present of a silver medal and designations of my state and war commander's offices, as

173

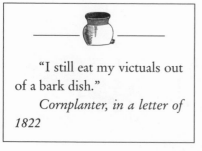

"I still eat my victuals out of a bark dish."
*Cornplanter, in a letter of 1822*

well as arms and ammunition and other things which represented the number of offices which I held. Thus, I was qualified by the Six Nations and by Washington.

After the stipulations of the treaty were completed and other business done that we were authorized to do, we started for home. Washington gave us a ticket to go up the river on a schooner, or great canoe, as far as Albany. There, we stopped one day. Washington had also given us a draft on some treasury of one hundred dollars in money. With the assistance of the Oneida Indians' agent, we obtained the one hundred dollars in money, and started on toward home and traveled on as fast as we could conveniently go. We made no more stops—only nights—till we arrived at Buffalo Creek, where we made our homes now that the bloody wars were over and it grew cold in the eastern part of the United States. And the Indians then commenced to make homes according to our forms, rules, and customs in all quarters within the boundaries before recognized.

Bark tray

## CHAPTER TEN

# "They Gave Us Poison in Return"

*In the Treaty of Fort Stanwix and later treaties, the New York Iroquois acknowledged the United States' dominion over the lands north and west of the Ohio River. To some, it looked as though the Iroquois had given away the lands of their western cousins, other Iroquoian peoples. In the midst of this difficult situation, the United States government put pressure on the Seneca and others to act as envoys to the western Indians.*

*Chainbreaker and his fellow ambassadors met with Washington in Philadelphia's new Congress Hall (called "the courthouse" by Chainbreaker) adjacent to the Pennsylvania Statehouse. Some probably rode in Washington's cream-colored French coach ornamented with cupids and flowers, which regularly carried the first president from his lodgings on Market Street to Congress Hall. (Chainbreaker says:* "Washington was with us—when we went into the courthouse.")

*But there was a flip side to Philadelphia's glossy public life, especially for visitors fresh from simpler, more isolated communities. Disease lurked along the streets of the eighteenth-century city. There were other dangers, too. Within a few years of the 1792 visit, the Seneca Chief, Farmer's Brother, would complain bitterly about Philadelphia's taverns, brothels, and gambling dens, which had corrupted his grandson, a student in the city.*

 Washington sent for us to come to his council at Pittsburgh [*actually Philadelphia*]; it was in the year 1792. Supposing it was for the purpose of associating [*making allies of*] the western Indians, we appointed a delegation. Seven chiefs were appointed, and one hundred and fifty warriors engaged to go with us to guard us from dangers. While we were making preparation to go, a messenger arrived from Canada; the Indians of Canada wished us to visit them. But, as for us, we could not go, for we had just engaged to accept the invitation of General Washington. We wished Brant to go with us, and sent for him by his own messenger, who went back to Canada; Brant was to be present or appear in this country within ten days. He appeared on the eighth day from the time we sent for him. He was then ready to go, with twenty-five more warriors at his side, so making in all one hundred and seventy-five warriors and eight chiefs.

We started about the middle of the summer. Before we came to the small village called Erie, fifteen more Indians overtook us who engaged to go with us. There were twelve Onondagas, two Tuscaroras, one Cayuga—with this addition making one hundred and ninety-nine souls from the State of New York.

We traveled the same old path we used to travel on the way to Pittsburgh, and it took us several days to reach there [*Philadelphia*]. After we came within three miles of the city, we camped out in the middle of the day to retire there till we learned more from Washington or from some of his commissioners about the purpose and objects of calling us together with him.

After we had eaten our dinners, Uncle Cornplanter sent me—and some others to go with me—downtown to see Washington. That afternoon when we came to the public house, I had to show my paper which recommended me and which requested an interview with Washington. The landlord told us which house Washington was in, so we went on to see him. I had a young white man for an interpreter. When we came to the house where the man had directed us to go, a well-armed man was standing at the door. I asked my interpreter to ask the doorkeeper whether Washington was in the house. The doorkeeper wanted to know what we wanted of him. I told the man in reply that I wanted to see Washington on business. We were soon called into the house and saw Washington, and we were glad to see each other. He asked me how many were in our company. I answered him, "One hundred and ninety-nine souls, delegates of the Five Nations, have come here at your express request."

"Died, in this city, on Monday last, Mr. Peter Jaquette, one of the principal Sachems of the Oneida Nation of Indians . . . The corpse was followed by six of the chiefs as mourners, succeeded by all the Warriors now in this city—the reverend Clergy of all denominations—the Secretary of War, and the Gentlemen of the War Department— Officers of the Federal Army, and of the Militia— and a number of Citizens. The concourse assembled on this occasion, is supposed, to have amounted to more than 10,000 persons."

*The Federal Gazette and Philadelphia Daily Advertiser, March 24, 1792*

"Yesterday the Chiefs and Warriors of the Five Nations assembled at the State House, and were welcomed to the city of Philadelphia, in an address delivered by the Governor . . . The room in which they assembled was mentioned as the ancient council chamber in which their ancestors and our's, had often met to brighten the chain of friendship; and this circumstance, together with the presence of a great part of the beauty of the city had an evident effect upon the feelings of the Indians."

*The Federal Gazette and Philadelphia Daily Advertiser, March 27, 1792*

"Last Monday evening, the Indian Chiefs, now in this city, entertained a number of the citizens with a sight of their festive dances. Their music on these occasions, is chiefly vocal, accompanied with the beat of a small drum."

*The Federal Gazette and Philadelphia Daily Advertiser, March 30, 1792*

"Very well," said he. "Be contained [*contain yourselves/relax*]. In three days, I will meet with you at the courthouse at nine o'clock AM." He then gave us orders on a provision store to get all we wanted to eat. So we went out, after we had finished talking, and went to the provision store and got flour and pork, tea, chocolate and sugar—all we could carry on our backs—and started for our camp.

Back at the camp, some of the boys had gone out to the woods to hunt fowl for us to eat for supper. So we enjoyed ourselves very well, and during the three days, our health was good.

At the expiration of the three days, we went up at the appointed hour. There were several carriages that met us on the way, for chiefs had to ride as well as any gentlemen ["any gentlemanship"], though our clothes were dirty. The carriages stopped at a clothing store; there we each obtained clothes.

After we had obtained new dress, we went on to the courthouse. Washington was then with us when we went into the courthouse. We occupied almost one half of the house. Washington wanted the chiefs to sit together face to face [*with the whites*]. The Seneca chiefs were seated by themselves; we were five of us, chiefs of the Seneca Nation.

Washington asked the names to be called out. So we went on to tell: Cornplanter, Red Jacket, Chainbreaker, Captain Strong, and Young King, Chief Warriors of the Senecas; Joseph Brant of the Mohawks, and Gr Go Da Nr Yeh of the Onondagas, and the two Chiefs of the Tuscarora Nation, and the Cayuga Chief of their nation— I cannot say what their English names were. Our men were seated behind us.

"The Indian Chiefs, now in this capital, have made their visit hither (it is said) in consequence of an invitation by Col. Pickering, Superintendent of Indian affairs, on behalf of the President of the United States . . ."

*Philadelphia National Gazette, March 29, 1792*

"Red Jacket was at that time about 30 or 35 years of age, of middle height, well-formed, with an intelligent countenance and a fine eye, and was a fine-looking man. He was the most graceful public speaker I have ever known; his manner was at the same time both dignified and easy; he was fluent, and at times, witty and sarcastic; he was quick and ready at reply; he pitted himself against Colonel Pickering, whom he sometimes foiled in argument. The Colonel would sometimes become irritated, and lose his temper; then Red Jacket would be delighted . . ."

*Thomas Morris, 1770- 1849, son of the Philadelphia banker, Robert Morris, in a diary account of another council held two years later*

Washington called the meeting to order and said to us, "I have called upon you for assistance in making peace and a treaty with the Western Indians of several tribes of different nations of Indians, for they are determined to continue to war with us. We do not want to shed any more blood with them, if possible. I sent a small company to make a treaty with these nations, but they have refused to receive the offer. They destroyed the company, and but a few escaped. I therefore thought I would have you try and see whether you could make peace with them, without any more fighting and bloodshed. If they receive your offer, come back to me. I will appoint a commissioner to make a treaty with them and be at peace with them—with no more war amongst the North American peoples, but peace with all the nations.

"I will give you a letter for them with written stipulations and with the United States seal, and I will furnish you with all necessary to take along with you. You won't suffer on my account, trying to make peace with every nation of Indians you come to. If they threaten you, get out of their way if you can. If you can't get out of their way, you must defend yourselves and be prepared for this purpose, or else give me notice as soon as possible if you require more men to get along with. I will send you

"We used sometimes to see a dozen Indians—sometimes 50 and sometimes 100 together—passing from here [Owego] to Tioga Point, Chenango Point, or Cayuga Lake . . . Some of them were Onondagas, some Cayugas, some Senecas. They often used to speak of Brant. He was their great man. The squaws used to delight to speak of him."

*Jesse McQuigg, speaking of the early 1790s*

men—as many as you want—and a naval force. This is all I have to say at present. If you want more things, let me know."

After he had finished talking, we consulted with each other, and we concluded to hold a council by ourselves. So Brant rose and said unto Washington that we would give him an answer the next day in the afternoon. So the meeting was adjourned.

After we had arrived at our camps, we then held a private meeting concerning the request by Washington. We all agreed we would obey him as an act of friendship. And we thought that it was our duty to make peace amongst the human race—our own red-colored men—and we thought that we might be able to make peace with the

"... the religious system of the Iroquois taught the existence of the Great Spirit Ha-wen-ne-yu; it also recognized the personal existence of an Evil Spirit Ha-ne-go-ate-geh, the Evil-Minded ... As the Good Spirit created men and all useful animals, and products of the earth, so the Evil Spirit created all monsters, poisonous reptiles, and noxious plants."

*Lewis Henry Morgan*

"Cornplanter informed me that when a young man, he was a great Hunter, and often thought of the Great Spirit, who made the wild beasts, and all things and to be sure he always had very good luck he said."

*Henry Simmons, Jr., Quaker missionary to the Seneca in 1796–1800*

help of the Great Spirit. For in every case, God is able to help to do good.

The next day, we went down to Pittsburgh [*Philadelphia*] at the hour we were to meet Washington at the courthouse, we found him on hand. Cornplanter then stood and said in answer that we would go where he ordered us to go—if there was danger or no danger. We would do the best, according to our abilities, to do good to every nation we might talk with and to declare peace and our desire to shed blood no more. About all this we felt doubtful—about the Western Nations granting us this peace. But if they did not receive our desires, it would not be a fault which could be laid on our heads. We also wished to go as soon as we could ready ourselves, and to come back again as soon as possible and to bring the news from them. We would act as faithful servants, et cetera.

Washington then rose and said, "I feel happy that you have accepted my wishes. I will furnish you all the

Seneca man

necessaries to take along with you—as I told you before, money and provisions. And if you want to sail downstream, I will furnish you boats to go down as far as you see fit, any time you are ready to start. You will be supplied with all things before your departure.

"Within three hours, the stipulations will be ready for you to take along with you to show these Indians, whatever nations you meet with—as I told you yesterday. And if you want any more arms, I will give orders on gun shops, and you can get what you want, or I will go with you."

Brant requested Washington to go with us to the shop, so not much more was said, only we all went downstairs with Washington and he led us to the gun shops. Red Jacket was next to Washington as we went along the sidewalk; I was far behind. After the chiefs obtained all they wanted, I went in. Washington asked me why I was not alongside of him when he went in—that I might have had my choice before so many guns were taken. I told him I did not want to put myself too far forward, for I was younger than the rest of the chiefs. He took my hand and led me to another shop and took his own choice of two good pistols and a rifle to give me—and all that belonged to the rifle, and a sword. And Captain Cass [*Jonathan Cass, 1753–1830, with Sullivan in 1779, appointed Captain in United States Army in 1790*], while we were in the shop, he handed me five dollars in pieces [*coins*].

The chiefs and warriors satisfied their wants and returned to the courthouse. The written stipulation, or

"Bushes were struck up and wove at the top together to make something like a tent to protect us. This the Indians helped us do, in which they were very skillful."

*Jane Strope Whitaker in her account of events of 1778*

description of our object, was about done. Brant, Cornplanter and myself went in and took the paper, and we went back to the camp for the night.

The next morning we started downtown, to go on down the river. On our way going into the town, three captains met us to let us know where to find the boats for us to ride down on. On Monongahela's shores[1] there were five boats ready for us and able to hold about two hundred and twenty men with their baggage.

So we started; it took us several days before we got down to Little Muskingum River, and we went upon that river several miles. We drew up ["placed"] our boat and camped out there three days before we pursued on after the Indians' trail. Yet, we saw no Indian families or hunting men during our first day's travel from this place—we expecting to see them or some Indian settlements along the edge of the prairies, some distance from the River Muskingum.

We traveled something like fifteen miles the following day before we came to the Indians' settlement—eight families together in one place. It appeared there were two distinct nations joined together, wandering about their country. As we approached them, the squaws came out of

---

[1] Confusingly, this is a Pittsburgh location.

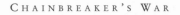

Seneca woman

their tents and met us in friendship. They wanted us to roast corn or have supper with them and stay until their men returned from hunting. We considered the effect of their influence in communicating our object, so, with good manners, we built tents [*of brush*] for the night alongside of their tents.

We soon saw their men coming home, during the time our men were fixing tents for us, and it looked as though we might have a rain that night. I stayed with the nearest neighbor to these strangers [*in the tent nearest to those of the strangers*]. I wished that I could speak their language,

"Gononkgoes, the Big Breast, is a gigantic woman whose breasts hang down like pillows. She roams the earth looking for lovers who sit close together in the dark. If they make one remark that seems to be improper in their love making, or if they stay at their love making too long, she leans over them, catching their faces beneath her breasts and smothering them. Then she stands upright, still holding the smothered lovers to her bosom, and walking to a cliff, leans over and drops them into the dark depths below."

*Seneca myth, related by Arthur C. Parker*

that I might have courted a squaw whom I took a liking to. The trouble was I could not understand what she said to me. She appeared to feel the same way about me when she was talking with me; she used a very friendly way with me. I wanted to know whether she was married or promised or not, but the trouble was, we could not understand each other—what we were saying about it. I felt desirous to learn something about her, for she was the handsomest I had ever seen, even among my own people. I asked Captain Hudson to go and talk with her, if he could understand their language. I told him, in secret, that I would like to marry her, if it could be done without interfering with our business and camping, and if she wanted to go with us on our journey and then home.

During the conversation with Hudson, this young squaw's father came into our tent. He pointed at me with his forefinger and wanted me to come over to their tent. I felt concern about it right off, and wanted to know what was meant by calling me to their tent. I asked Captain

Horn rattle used in the Seneca Bear Dance

Hudson to go along with me. It was not but a very few steps between our tent and theirs. After we had sat down in their tent, Captain Hudson talked with the old man. I supposed that this tribe of Indians, they were what they call Osage Indians [*probably Shawnee—see Editor's Note*]. Hudson could understand but little of their language; most of the conversation they had by motions of their hands. We all got along that way to find out the meaning of what we said to them and what they said to us. At last, we understood that they wanted us to go to a certain place that evening to show us their council tent, and that

"It was the duty of the young Indian man who wished to marry to inform his parents of his desire, stating the name of the maiden . . . If the friends and relations were willing, the son was permitted to offer his suit."

*Passamaquoddy Wampum Records*

". . . my sisters told me that I must go and live with one of them, whose name was She-nin-jee. Not daring to cross them, or disobey their commands, with a great degree of reluctance I went; and Sheninjee and I were married according to Indian custom."

*Mary Jemison*

some of our company might go with us.

I went back to our fire and called several of our men to go along with us to see these Osage dancing tents; so they started with us. When we came to the long tent, it was made of the stems of weeds—something like ten-foot lengths of these stems—and covered with the same stuff. The Osage chief, he made signs that they wanted to dance that night; we agreed some of us might come to see.

"Roasted corn, Gani-ste-da. This was the husked ear of green corn baked in hot embers . . . one of the old methods was to dig a long trench and place the ears across two slender green saplings and allow the heat of the hot coals to cook the corn . . ."

*Arthur C. Parker*

When we returned to the tent where this young squaw lived, I talked with the old man about his daughter, by signs asking him whether she was married or promised to her husband. As near as I could learn, she was not married and never had been. I said no more to him or to her about it, till I could ask Uncle Cornplanter his advice about my having this young squaw as a lover. He said to me that I had better let her alone and speak no more about it—the marriage. I felt sorrow.

Red Jacket was then speaking, and notifying the companions that as soon as we arose in the morning, we would communicate with these Osage Indians concerning our object of making peace with all the Indian nations, and would communicate Washington's wishes to fight no more and also the fact that we were sent by him for this business. This night we had a great deal of green corn to roast by the fireside.

Some of us went back to the dance, as they wanted us to come. We went on to their dance and saw them perform—differently from the way we do and with different regulations. They seemed to pay stricter attention to the managers of the dancing party. And the squaws also seemed to have as much to do as any man in regulating the female party—as much as the man who commanded them

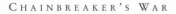

during their dance. We stayed three hours at their dance, we wanted to go back; we wanted to sleep in order to rise early in the morning.

The next morning when the sun was three hours high, we gathered together. Brant took the paper and read it to them, by signs and motions, in order for them to understand the language of the paper. And they understood it well and gave answer that they would go home to meet in council for the purpose of fully understanding. After this meeting closed, we took up our baggage and started on our course. The Osage Indians started on after us. We did not see any more Indians that day.

The next day in the afternoon, we came to a thick settlement of Indians where we

"On the first day of this festival [Green Corn] . . . the Feather dance, the thanksgiving address, with the burning of tobacco, and three or four other dances, made up the principal religious exercises . . . the great Feather dance, O-sto-weh-go-wa . . . was the most splendid, graceful and remarkable . . .

"The dancers were usually nude down to the waist, with the exception of ornaments upon their arms and necks, thus exposing their well-formed chests, finely rounded arms, and their smooth, evenly colored skins, of a clear and brilliant copper color . . ."
*Lewis Henry Morgan*

"I remember them having the Green Corn Dance and the Maple Dance."
*Jane Strope Whitaker*

made a stop, and Brant, Red Jacket, and Cornplanter went amongst the different nations to inquire whether an interpreter of different languages could be found. They found one of the Wyandot Indians who could speak our language well. They also found Kickapoos who could understand Wyandots, Chippewas who could understand Kickapoos, Potawatomis who could understand Chippewas, and Osages who could understand Potawatomis. All of the Thirteen Nations talk and use different languages. We had to transfer [*translate*], one to another, in order for all to understand what we had to say to them in council.

Notice was given out amongst them for a council to be opened by us the next day in the morning; yet, they did not know for what object. Several of their chiefs came to us and made enquiries as to our object and as to what we intended to do. They expected to embrace and carry out new plans for warfare, and they were quite friendly to us and gave us venison and cornbread to eat for our supper. After supper, they began to tell of their wars with the whites and how they had managed at such battles which had taken place, how long they had fought and how many times within the year, how many they had killed and how many of their own had lost their lives, and where, and what nation made up the greatest part of their number, and which the least of their number, and who was the bravest man amongst the officers and who had been the most successful at different times during the previous eight years.

The next day, about ten o'clock AM, the people began to gather together. The chief had ordered one of their men to build a fire near a big elm tree, which shaded some fine green grass under the tree. The old chief called upon the interpreters to arrange their seats

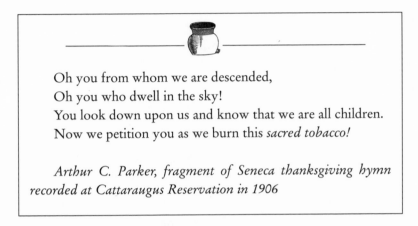

Oh you from whom we are descended,
Oh you who dwell in the sky!
You look down upon us and know that we are all children.
Now we petition you as we burn this *sacred tobacco!*

*Arthur C. Parker, fragment of Seneca thanksgiving hymn recorded at Cattaraugus Reservation in 1906*

between the Six Nations and the Thirteen Nations. There was one Mohawk interpreter, one Wyandot, one Kickapoo, one Chippewa, one Potawatomi, and one Osage, and these were the several languages which they could speak and understand. They enabled us to understand all the communications.

Red Jacket arose and said unto the public, "Friends and brothers, it was the will of the Great God that we should meet together this day. He orders all things, for his kindness has enabled us to hold this council. He has taken his garment from before the sun, and so caused it to shine with brightness on us. Our eyes are opened that we might see clearly; our ears are unstopped that we might be able to understand distinctly the words spoken. For all these favors, we thank the Great God and him only."

Joseph Brant rose and took the Declaration of Peace and read it to them through the interpreters—to one, to another, to one after the other—in order that it be understood by those of every tongue. After reading it through,

"After his [Washington's] death, he was mourned by the Iroquois as a benefactor of their race, and his memory was cherished with reverence and affection. A belief was spread abroad among them, that the Great Spirit had received him into a celestial residence upon the plains of heaven, the only white man whose noble deeds had entitled him to this heavenly favor. Just by the entrance of heaven is a walled enclosure, the ample grounds within which are laid out with avenues and shaded walks. Within is a spacious mansion, constructed in the fashion of a fort . . . the illustrious inmate . . . walks to and fro in quiet meditation. But no word ever passes his lips. Dressed in his uniform, and in a state of perfect felicity, he is destined to remain through eternity in the solitary enjoyment of the celestial residence prepared for him by the Great Spirit."

*Lewis Henry Morgan*

he then spoke on behalf of the Six Nations: "We speak as one united voice of the Six Nations. On the battlefield, in the forests, and in the valleys, the wars are now closed with America, and there is made a reserve, a large tract of land sufficient for all the Six Nations to remain on, with hunting grounds, trapping ponds, and fishing rivers. We have been deceived by Great Britain in the transaction of the bloody wars with our white neighbors of North America, and we have found that we will have to exchange fathers. Hereafter, we will have one on this island for our protection, if we submit to entering a treaty with all nations for peace and to war no more and to shed blood no more and—if God grants—to give us future prosperity.

"We had better think about what must be done to continue the war against the whites, and then drop it, where we now are, and save lives and keep this war from frightening our women and children. We have been sent here to talk with all of you to see whether you will agree with us. We feel desirous that you agree with us without controversy amongst you. But whatever you give us in answer, we will return with the tidings to Washington.

"I repeat, cover up your war fires to see them no more! We have created a new father, near at home, for our protection against foreigners who might come—if there is any danger of another contest between Great Britain and America hereafter. We consider this the object: to settle up all the difficulties, afflictions, severe feelings, and sore hearts. We said to Washington—we asked each other— what have we done to deserve such severe chastisement? Our hatchets and tomahawks and knives were buried under the ground, not to be raised against any nation any more. But we raised them by order of Great Britain, for we helped him, and he has now given up to Washington.

"Washington brought kindness. He asked us for a settlement to fight no more immediately after the British were defeated and had delivered their red children to the American people to do as they saw fit with us—destroy us, or save us to be slaves, or set us free. We are yet free from bondage today, although we have not completed or closed with all the treaties we attended to with the Town Destroyer, that is, Washington. [*The Iroquois gave Washington this name following Sullivan's destructive campaign.*] We intend to finish what is undone with Washington and our Six Nations of Indians residing in the eastern part of the continent of America. I will now leave you to be your own judges concerning this."

One of the Osage chiefs got up and said, "We will consider the subject. We will return tomorrow morning, and you must remain until we return."

On the second day, about eight o'clock AM, we met together on the same ground. The fire had been built early in the morning. More people gathered at this assembly than the previous day. There were men, women, and children as far as I could see, for half a mile away in all directions, appearing to move towards the middle of the assembly. In an hour and a half's time, all were seated and quieted.

The old chief of the Osage Indians arose and said, "We are now ready to give you our view on the subject you set before us yesterday. God has given it to his western red children to unite once more. All are agreed of the Thirteen Nations and the thirteen different languages of the red men. God made us all; he made the earth, and the men upon it to multiply, and the animals—all given to his red children." He said no more and sat down.

Another one got up and said, "I am one of the Kickapoos, and war officer for several tribes of adjacent Indians. Friends and brothers, I ask you to let me have that stipulation read to us yesterday and intended for us to receive. I want it so that I may give you a short piece of work in answer." He made a few steps towards us to take the paper.

Brant rose; he said to us, "Shall we give up the written document to him? Red Jacket says 'yes.' I say 'no'—till we understand further." But then Brant, himself, thought it best to give up the written document to the warrior. He handed it to him. The warrior took it and stepped back to his place a few feet from the fireside. They passed a few words amongst themselves there.

He soon turned round towards us, and facing the Solato River [*Maumee River*], at the meeting of the waters, said, "Brothers, this paper was written by Town Destroyer, and we also understand that he wants to make a treaty with the red man to fight no more, for he has already settled with the redcoat man. We also understand that you, the Six Nations, have already settled with Washington.

"I call you very cowardly red men. You may tell Washington that I have taken this paper and cast it into the fire. We will continue to stand firmly to protect our lands and our rights. We will die before we give up to our enemy. We have a feeling about our people and our rights, which God has given us. We feel they are honored in the sight of the Almighty.

"Remember how the whites served us at the time the first white man discovered our island—how they cheated

"The hunter selected the choice pieces of venison, and having removed the bone, and dried and cured the flesh before a fire, he packed it in small bark barrels, and thus carried it . . . upon his back. It was so much reduced in weight and bulk by the process of curing, that a hunter could thus transport, with ease, the substance of a dozen deer."

*Lewis Henry Morgan*

us, not only cheated us in trade, but even in all policy. They found us ignorant. We thought that they were a good people, and that they were very small. And we had mercy upon them and gave them good things. They gave us poison in return!

"You deserve punishment! You ought to be cut off for falling in with the white man! But we conclude that you should go back home and mind your own business, and we will do the same." So he had no more to say.

The assembly arose. This afternoon, they looked as though they were enemies to us. So we got away the best way we could from this place and made for home, straight away to Franklin Creek. We made no stops before we reached Franklin—only nights and to get venison dried up for provision on the way, nothing else during several days travel, and nothing but venison to eat as we went along.

These Thirteen Nations of the Solato River had threatened our lives considerably before we left them. Cornplanter told them that we had not come there to fight with them, but if they saw fit, we would defend ourselves as far as we were able. But we were first desirous to get away without fighting.

After we came to Franklin Creek, we stayed to rest a few days, then started upon the creek and followed it till we reached up to what is now called Midville, and so on to Erie on the lake shore. We traveled along the lake shore to our homes at Buffalo. We all reached home save one man, who died on the way home.

CHAPTER ELEVEN

# "To Go West Once More"

Asecond trip west was ill fated in every way. As Chainbreaker relates, his party had to turn back before it reached the Maumee River. Cornplanter's party did reach the encampments of the western peoples, but there, was seized and imprisoned, and its members threatened with death. After their release, many died on the trip homeward. As Emily Tallchief (18??-19??) great-great-granddaughter of Cornplanter, told the story: "The delegation went through Sandusky into the farther west. There Cornplanter called a council and said, 'We must be peaceful with the white men and cease tormenting them.' Now the tribe was a very fierce one and was very angry that Cornplanter advised peace. They mixed poison with the food which they served the delegation and a number died. Cornplanter also was made severely ill."

*The western nations would not make peace until 1796, the*
*year the British ceded all military and trading posts in the area.*

We then had nothing more to do with this counciling business. We only felt surprise to think we had been involved in it. And as our object was rejected by the western Indians, our people thought it best to let it rest till the next spring—in June of 1793.

At that time, the United States Commissioners opened a council at Black Rock near Buffalo for the purpose of communicating with the western Indians; once more, they wanted us to go to the western Indians to make peace with them. Several tribes of Indians kept annoying their enemies—the whites—after the Six Nations had made a treaty with Washington.

At about the same time, our people were making preparation—a small part of each nation—to go over to Canada. Upon this, Washington would have us, the Six Nations of Iroquois, to go west once more to make peace. So we took consideration of the desires and the request of Washington, and the consultation of the Six Nations was that we would try once more. So we returned the request with a favorable answer. The Commissioner presented a written document describing the business and the peace stipulation of Washington. So this was finished and completed on the part of the United States and the New York Indians, and it was agreed they would ready themselves within a month. Thus the meeting closed.

The Indian people who had been swayed to go over to Canada, they were about ready to start. But it so happened that Washington wished us to go to the upper part of Lake Erie, and this put them off from going over at present. I was then ready at any time I should be called. As for the rest of the Indians, the generals of the Six Nations agreed to let those remain behind who were engaged to go over to Canada.

About twenty days after this, the company readied itself to go; two hundred men of the company started. I took fifty men of the company under my command, John Decker took fifty men in his command, and Cornplanter and Brant took charge of the rest of the company, what we called the common company. Those in the first two commands were the choice men, generally good hunters who supported the whole of their companions on the journey's way.

This type of doll was made in obedience to a dream
and cast aside to carry away some malady.

Our journey took the old path which we used to travel some time ago and where we knew every part of the country. When we came to French Creek near the Allegheny River, about one hundred of us stopped for the purpose of dressing deerskins in order to make our moccasins. We, the hunter fellows, went to the river. As we approached the village of Franklin, we came across a large drove of elks. We pursued them and killed about fifteen of them. We camped out there to dress our venison and dry it so it could be carried with us easily on the way. We had to stay till the other company overtook us so that we might have help carrying our venison along, as we expected, whenever we did go, not to stop again till we had reached the Upper Sandusky.

We stayed at this place two days before the other company reached us. On the third day, we all joined together again and went on towards the headwaters of what is now called Big Beaver Creek. Our calculations called for us to take a straight course towards the place of our appointment. On our way, towards evening, we came across several Indians already camped out for some time. As we approached them, about ten or fifteen rods from them, two Indians began to run. As we continued towards them, very soon others ran, one after the other.

I began to step swiftly towards them. When we came to their fire, four stayed near the fireside, sitting on the ground. We surrounded them; one of our company took their guns and other arms. They appeared willing to be taken as prisoners of war. But they soon whispered to one another, and in an instant, they jumped against our men and cut through and ran with all their might. We fired at them; two fell and two got away from us. I followed a short distance, till I was satisfied they were not wounded or hurt, and then wheeled back again.

As I was returning, the first thing I knew, a gun fired to my left. They made three shots at me, which never touched, and they gave Indian whoops and ran out. I fired

Common type of husk doll

at them; I broke one fellow's leg. He fell as I came up to him. He spoke the Delaware language, which I cannot understand. When I examined the wound on his leg, I could discover no cure. I just laid my hatchet over his head, and said nothing more about it. I dragged him towards the other ones and buried them that evening and retired for the night.

These Indians—as near as I could learn, since the one spoke to me in the Delaware language—I considered that they must have been Delaware Indians from the west. They were enemies to us, and they knew it, too, else they would not have run as they did. I supposed that they had been at this place some time. They had considerable good venison on hand, so we had a good dish out of it for our supper. We also supposed that they had been on their way to attack the country families towards Pittsburgh. We stayed two nights at this place, and then our captain ordered us to return back.

One year after the warriors' return from the West:

"Oct. 30 [1794]—After dinner, John Parish and myself rode to view the Farmer's Brother encampment, which contained about five hundred Indians. They are located by the side of a brook, in the woods; having built about seventy or eighty huts, by far the most commodious and ingeniously made of any I have seen. The principal materials are bark and boughs of trees, so nicely put together as to keep the family dry and warm. The women as well as the men seemed to be mostly employed. In this camp there are a large number of pretty children, who, in all the activity and buoyancy of health, were diverting themselves according to their fancy. The vast number of deer they have killed, since coming here, which they cut up and hang around their huts, inside and out, to dry, together with the rations of beef which they draw daily, give the appearance of plenty to supply the few wants to which they are subjected.

The ease and cheerfulness of every countenance, and the delightfulness of the afternoon, which these inhabitants of the woods seemed to enjoy with a relish far superior to those who are pent up in crowded and populous cities, all combined to make this the most pleasant visit I have yet made to the Indians, and induced me to believe that before they became acquainted with white people, and were infected with their vices, they must have been as happy a people as any in the world. In returning to our quarters, we passed by the Indian council, where Red Jacket was displaying his oratory to his brother chiefs, on the subject of Colonel Pickering's proposals."

*William Savary, 1750–1804, Quaker missionary, from his diary account written at Canandaigua, New York*

# AFTERWORD

The happy camp at Canandaigua offered a last flickering view of good times among the Seneca. Overall, the 1790s were a low point in the history of the Seneca Nation. Demoralized by the loss of lands through federal treaty and to dishonest private purchasers, the Seneca clustered in reservation villages that soon became "Slums in the Wilderness," in the words of one writer. The men, without their usual occupations of hunting and warfare, drank and brawled. Malnourished young people sickened with tuberculosis, and their frightened parents often blamed witchcraft and the supernatural. A true witch fever swept the desperate villages in the last years of the century. One of Hah Na I Sah's earliest memories was the terrible execution of a handsome and intelligent young woman as a witch. (The executioners forced red-hot sticks down her throat.)

Chainbreaker and his uncle, Cornplanter, played important roles in the rescue and revival of their people. Cornplanter welcomed Quaker missionaries, who encouraged the Seneca men to help their women in the fields and to adopt some European methods of agriculture, especially the use of plows and teams of horses. Chainbreaker championed the Seneca prophet, Handsome Lake, one of his uncles, who preached a new, moral code that specifically addressed many problems of reservation life. Chainbreaker was actually one of the first to reach Handsome Lake's side following the prophet's visionary faint.

During the War of 1812, Chainbreaker fought along with other New York Seneca for the American side. He even led a memorable war dance through the streets of Buffalo at the outset of the war. In the years after 1815, an already-existing division between the two great leaders, Cornplanter and Red Jacket, hardened. Basically, Cornplanter wanted the Seneca to draw closer to the white world; Red Jacket took a more adversarial position towards that world. Chainbreaker came down on Red Jacket's side in this battle for the hearts and minds of the Seneca. He was a traditionalist, strongly bonded to his own people and culture. While he agreed to the 1823 sale of the Gardeau Reserve, named for Mary Jemison's husband, on the Genesee River, he resisted and protested the 1838 sale of land south of Buffalo to the Ogden Company via a charter with many dubious signatures.

At about this time, the late 1830s, a boy living near Cold Spring attended a Seneca funeral on the Cattaraugus Reserve where he saw and heard the old warrior: "The deceased was a young Indian of about twenty-one years of age who had fallen a victim to consumption. After the coffin had been lowered into the grave, the father of the young man dropped a bow and arrows down beside it. The good Governor [Chainbreaker] then mounted the pile of mould which had been thrown out of the grave — his tall form towering perfectly erect, his whitened locks streaming in the breeze — when he made a speech, which, though I could not understand a single word of it, made an impression on my mind which I shall never forget. He was very grave and the attitudes with which the Indians listened bore evidence of the great estimation in which he was held."[1]

In 1850, the historian Lyman Draper spent two days with the sachem, gathering intelligence on Revolutionary War battles. Draper noted Chainbreaker's fine appearance, but nothing more of a personal nature beyond one glimpse: "Blacksnake [Chainbreaker] seems to have more reverence for Red Jacket than for any other Indian. Has one of the Weir engraved portraits of him framed, hanging up in his room (with others, Washington, Jackson, Scott, Worth, and [illegible]) and often took it down, and would smilingly show it to me, saying, "Jack-Et." Says the engraving (same as in Stone's works) is a good one."[2]

A few years after Draper's visit, and a full ten years after Chainbreaker gave his narrative to Hah Na I Sah, the aged sachem performed a last service for his people. In 1856, he supplied important testimony in a law case—testimony that preserved reservation land, the Oil Spring Tract in Pennsylvania, for the Seneca. The ninety-seven-year-old sachem spoke and also produced an old map, long saved and guarded, to prove his nation's claim.

---

[1] Letter of Charles Aldrich to Lyman Draper, dated Jan. 12, 1850. "Draper Manuscripts," Wisconsin Historical Society, Series 16F, p. 228.
[2] Conversation with Gov. Blacksnake," Draper Manuscripts," State Historical Society of Wisconsin, Series 4S, p. 75.

# NOTES

Most of the uncredited engravings that appear throughout the book were drawn from Lewis Henry Morgan's 1851 volume, *League of the Ho-De-No-Sau-Nee, Iroquois*, with a few derived from Arthur C. Parker's early-twentieth-century New York State Museum Bulletins: "Iroquois Uses of Maize and Other Food Plants"; "The Code of Handsome Lake, the Seneca Prophet"; and "The Constitution of the Five Nations."

Chapter One:
"No People Can Live More Happy"

p. 32.   Lewis Henry Morgan, *League of the Ho-De-No-Sau-Nee, Iroquois* (Rochester, NY: Sage & Brother, Publishers, 1851).

p. 34.   Thomas McKenney, *History of the Indian Tribes of North America* (New York, NY: Scribner & Sons, 1870), entry on "Corn Plant"; Wisconsin Historical Society, "Draper Manuscripts," Series F, no. 17, p. 220.

p. 35.   Morgan, *op.cit.*, pp. 315-18.

p. 37.   Morgan, pp. 367-8.

p. 38.   James E. Seaver, *A Narrative of the Life of Mrs. Mary Jemison.* (1824; reprinted with introduction by June Namias. Norman, OK: University of Oklahoma Press, 1992).

p. 39.   Arthur C. Parker, "Constitution of the Five Nations," in W. N. Fenton, ed. *Parker on the Iroquois* (Syracuse, NY: Syracuse University Press, 1968) p. 30.

p. 41.   Barbara Graymont, *The Iroquois in the American Revolution* (Syracuse, NY: Syracuse University Press, 1972) p. 106.

p. 43.   Morgan, p. 364.

p. 44.   Graymont, *op.cit.*, p. 48.

p. 45.   "Draper Manuscripts," *op.cit.*, Series F, no. 17, p. 62.

p. 46.   John N. Hubbard, *Sketches of Border Adventures in the Life and Times of Major Moses Van Campen, a Surviving Soldier of the Army of the Revolution* (Bath, NY: 1842) pp. 272-3.

p. 47.   Seaver, *op.cit.*, p. 97.

## Chapter Two:
## "We Will Go and Attend the Father"

p. 53.   Seaver, p. 98.
p. 57.   Morgan, pp. 265-6.
p. 58.   Morgan, p. 387.
p. 59.   Seaver, p. 107; McKenney, *op.cit.*
p. 60.   Parker, "Constitution of the Five Nations," *op.cit.*, p. 42.

## Chapter Three:
## "Few White Men Escaped from Us"

p. 64.   Seaver, p. 99.
p. 66.   William Campbell, *Annals of Tryon County; or, the Border Warfare of New York, during the Revolution* (New York, NY: Baker & Scribner, 1849) p. 99.
p. 68.   "Draper Manuscripts," Series F, no. 17, p. 34.
p. 69.   Seaver, p. 100.

## Chapter Four:
## "It Was Done in Honor"

p. 72.   Morgan, p. 322.
p. 73.   Morgan, p. 264; "Draper manuscripts," Series F, no. 17, p. 42.
p. 74.   Seaver, p. 78.
p. 77.   Morgan, p. 318; George H. Harris, "The Life and Captivity of Horatio Jones," *Publication of the Buffalo Historical Society*, ed. Frank H. Severance (Buffalo, NY: Buffalo Historical Society, 1923) p. 417.

## Chapter Five:
## "I Killed Many"

p. 83.   "Draper Manuscripts," Series F, no. 17, p. 23.
p. 84.   Wyoming Historical and Geological Society, *The massacre of Wyoming. The acts of Congress for the defense of the*

*Wyoming Valley, Pennsylvania, 1776-1778: with the petitions of the sufferers by the massacre of July 3, 1778, for congressional aid* (Wilkes-Barre, PA: Printed for the Society, 1895) p. 51.

p. 86.  Wyoming Historical and Geological Society, *op.cit.*, p. 73, p. 51.

p. 87.  Wyoming Historical and Geological Society, p. 53.

p. 88.  Morgan, p. 338.

p. 91.  Parker, "Constitution of the Five Nations," p. 53.

p. 93.  Graymont, p. 180.

## Chapter Six:
### "The Danger Was Near at Hand"

p. 97.  Seaver, pp. 101-2.

p. 98.  Frederick Cook, ed., *Journals of the Military Expedition of Major-General John Sullivan Against the Six Nations of Indians in 1779 with Records of Centennial Celebrations* (Auburn, NY: Knapp, Peck & Thomson, 1887) p. 188.

p. 99.  Seaver, pp. 104-5.

p. 100.  Cook, *op.cit.*, pp. 307-8.

p. 102.  Cook, p. 308.

p. 103.  Morgan, p. 319; Seaver, p. 87.

p. 104.  Arthur C. Parker, "Iroquois Uses of Maize," in W. N. Fenton, ed., *Parker on the Iroquois, op.cit.*, p. 69.

p. 105.  Benson J. Lossing, *Pictorial Fieldbook of the American Revolution* (New York, NY: Harper & Bros, 1860) vol. 1, p. 225; Lossing, *op.cit.*

p. 106.  Cook, p. 17.

p. 108.  "Draper manuscripts," Series S, no. 4, p. 77.

p. 109.  Morgan, p. 376.

p. 110  Seaver, p. 105.

p. 111.  Seaver, p. 84.

## Chapter Seven:
### "Remember Me Who Rescued You"

p. 131.  Seaver, p. 75.

p. 133. William Walton, *A narrative of the captivity and sufferings of Benjamin Gilbert and his family. Who were surprised by the Indians and taken from their farm, on Mahoning creek, in Penn township, Northampton county, not far from where Fort Allen was built, on the frontier of Pennsylvania, in the spring of 1780 . . .* (Lancaster, PA: Privately printed, 1890), pp. 133-5.

p. 136. Parker, "Iroquois Uses of Maize," *op.cit.,* p. 76.

p. 138. Walton, *op.cit.,* p. 127.

Chapter Eight:
"We Won't Give Up Our Lands"

p. 140-1. Anthony Wallace, *The Death and Rebirth of the Seneca* (New York, NY: Vintage, 1972) p. 197.

p. 142. "Draper Manuscripts," Series F, no. 17, pp. 62-3.

p. 145. "Draper Manuscripts," Series F, no. 17, p. 38.

p. 146. "Draper Manuscripts," Series F, no. 17, pp. 43, 46.

p. 147. Parker, "Constitution of the Five Nations," p. 50.

p. 149. Parker, "Constitution of the Five Nations," p. 44.

p. 150. Harris, *op.cit.,* pp. 449-51.

p. 153. Morgan, p. 183.

p. 154. Morgan, p. 7.

p. 155. Morgan, p. 303.

Chapter Nine:
"The War Was Now Closed"

p. 160. Nelly K. Gordon, ed., *The Fort Dearborn Massacre written in 1814 by Lieutenant Linai T. Helm . . . with letters and narratives of contemporary interest* (Chicago, IL: Rand McNally, 1912).

p. 162. Francis Jennings et al., eds., *Iroquois Indians: A documentary history of the Six Nations and their league.* Microfilm (Woodbridge, CT: D'Arcy McNickle Center for the History of the American Indian and the Newberry Library, 1984) Reel 38, "April, 25, 1786."

p. 167. Jennings et al., *op.cit.*

p. 170. Harris, p. 423.

p. 171. Seaver, p. 107.

p. 174. McKenney, *op.cit.*

## Chapter Ten:
## "They Gave Us Poison in Return"

p. 178. Newspapers on microfilm, New York State Library, Albany.

p. 180. Newspapers on microfim, *op.cit.*; Francello, Joseph A., *The Seneca World of Ga-No-Say-Yeh* (*Peter Crouse, White Captive*) (Lanham, MD: University Press of America, 1980) p. 47.

p. 182. Morgan, p. 156; Francello, *op.cit.*, p. 56.

p. 185. "Draper Manuscripts," Series F, no. 17, p. 24.

p. 187. Arthur C. Parker, *Seneca Myths and Folk Tales* (Buffalo, NY: Buffalo Historical Society, 1923) p. 19.

p. 189. Parker, "Constitution of the Five Nations," pp. 123-4; Seaver, p. 81.

p. 190. Parker "Iroquois Uses of Maize," p. 78.

p. 191. Morgan, pp. 279-82; "Draper Manuscripts," Series F, no. 17, p. 35.

p. 193. Parker, "Code of Handsome Lake," in Fenton, *op.cit.*, p. 86.

p. 194. Morgan, pp. 178-9.

p. 197. Morgan, p. 346.

## Chapter Eleven:
## "To Go West Once More"

p. 202. *Transactions of the Buffalo Historical Society* (Buffalo, NY: Published by order of the Society, 1885) Appendix 19.

# ANNOTATED BIBLIOGRAPHY

Abler, Thomas, ed. *Chainbreaker: The Revolutionary War Memoirs of Governor Blacksnake as told to Benjamin Williams.* Lincoln, NB: University of Nebraska Press, 1989.

This work contains Hah Na I Sah/Williams' unedited manuscript (or actually a combination of two, near-identical versions which Hah Na I Sah/Williams gave to Draper), along with Abler's extensive notes on Chainbreaker and the events he describes. *Chainbreaker's War* draws upon Abler for its own brief introduction and editor's remarks, but does not follow Abler in every respect. While he identifies "General Duckey" as a loyalist officer named Richard McDonell or McDonald, this editor accepted Draper's view of the matter—that "Duckey" was Walter Butler, son of the loyalist Colonel John Butler.

Campbell, William. *Annals of Tryon County; or, the Border Warfare of New York, during the Revolution.* New York, NY: Baker & Scribner, 1849.

Campbell interviewed a number of veterans of the Oriskany battle (*Annals* was first published in 1831). Thus, the description of the Battle of Oriskany drawn from this volume represents a good second-hand account.

Cook, Frederick, ed. *Journals of the Military Expedition of Major-General John Sullivan Against the Six Nations of Indians in 1779 with Records of Centennial Celebrations.* Auburn, NY: Knapp, Peck & Thomson, 1887.

This collection has preserved a remarkable number of eyewitness accounts of Sullivan's campaign and other campaigns of 1779. It is the source of the remarks of Major General John Sullivan, Colonel Daniel Brodhead, and Lieutenant Erkuries Beatty.

Fenton, William N., ed. *Parker on the Iroquois: Iroquois Uses of Maize and Other Food Plants; The Code of Handsome Lake, the Seneca Prophet; The Constitution of the Five Nations.* Syracuse, NY: Syracuse University Press, 1968.

Arthur Caswell Parker was an anthropologist and museum curator of part-Seneca ancestry who was active from the early 1900s through the 1920s. This volume reprints three of his works, originally published as bulletins of the New York State Museum. In 1910 he visited the Six Nations Reserve on Grand River in Ontario where he was thrilled to find a flourishing traditional Iroquois society. There, he collected native manuscripts and edited them to create "The Constitution of the Five Nations." All of Parker's remarks on corn, and all excerpts from "The Constitution of the Five Nations," were drawn from this volume, as well as Parker's recording of the Seneca thanksgiving hymn and Emily Tallchief's story about Cornplanter. The single quotation from the "Passamaquoddy Wampum Records" is taken from Appendix A of "The Constitution of the Five Nations."

Francello, Joseph A. *The Seneca World of Ga-No-Say-Yeh (Peter Crouse, White Captive)*. Lanham, MD: University Press of America, 1980.
This work contains the excerpt from Henry Simmons, Jr.ss diary concerning Cornplanter (a typescript copy of the diary is held by the Pennsylvania State Archives, Harrisburg, PA) and the excerpt from Thomas Morris' "Personal Memoir" concerning Red Jacket (Volume 13 of "Henry O'Reilly Papers Pertaining to the Six Nations," New-York Historical Society, NYC, microfilm, 1948).

Gordon, Nelly K., ed. *The Fort Dearborn Massacre written in 1814 by Lieutenant Linai T. Helm . . . with letters and narratives of contemporary interest*. Chicago, IL: Rand McNally, 1912. "The capture by the Indians of little Eleanor Lytle" forms one chapter of this volume dealing mainly with later conflicts. Apparently included as an afterthought, the account has preserved a fascinating glimpse of "Big White Man," or Cornplanter.

Graymont, Barbara. *The Iroquois in the American Revolution*. Syracuse, NY: Syracuse University Press, 1972.
Along with Thomas Abler's *Chainbreaker: The Revolutionary War Memoirs of Governor Blacksnake*, this work supplied important background information for the introduction and notes of *Chainbreaker's War*. Curious readers may wish to turn to Graymont for a complete account of the Iroquois role in the Revolutionary War. *Chainbreaker's War* plucks three intriguing quotations from Graymont's pages: Sir William Johnson on the "Covenant Chain," General Philip Schuyler on the large appetites of the Iroquois at the

1776 council near Albany, and Colonel Thomas Hartley on Iroquois bravery in 1778.

There is perhaps one small flaw in Graymont's work. Her warm sympathy for the Iroquois causes her to dismiss, on very weak evidence, credible accounts from some wartime sufferers. See particularly the 1837 depositions of survivors of Wyoming concerning the presence of women with the Iroquois war bands.

Harris, George H. "The Life and Captivity of Horatio Jones." *Publication of the Buffalo Historical Society* (Frank H. Severance, ed.) Buffalo, NY: Buffalo Historical Society, 1903.

This account contains many glimpses of daily life among the eighteenth-century Seneca, including the two—of the house interior, and of the trip to the "pigeon grounds"—excerpted here.

Hubbard, John N. *Sketches of Border Adventures in the Life and Times of Major Moses Van Campen, a Surviving Soldier of the Army of the Revolution*. Bath, NY: 1842.

The source of the description of the "Turtle Dance."

Jennings, Francis, et al., eds. *Iroquois Indians: A documentary history of the Six Nations and their league*. Microfilm, Reel 38. Woodbridge, CT: D'Arcy McNickle Center for the History of the American Indian and the Newberry Library, 1984.

The letter of Richard Butler to George Washington concerning the Iroquois journey to Philadelphia and then the coach accident on the way to New York may be located on the reel by its date, April 25, 1786.

Lossing, Benson J. *Pictorial Fieldbook of the Revolution*. 2 vols. New York: Harper & Bros, 1860. Volume One contains Lossing's own description of Fort Niagara, as well as the quotation from Samuel De Veau's 1839 *Falls of Niagara* on the "unholy unions" at the fort.

McKenney, Thomas. *History of the Indian Tribes of North America*. New York, NY: Scribner & Sons, 1870.

All of the direct quotations from Cornplanter have been drawn from an 1822 letter written by the sachem to the Governor of Pennsylvania and reproduced, in part, by McKenney in his chapter on "Corn Plant."

Morgan, Lewis Henry. *League of the Ho-De-No-Sau-Nee, Iroquois.* Rochester, NY: Sage & Brother, Publishers, 1851.

This wonderfully full work of Victorian scholarship has provided the richest fund of "excerpts." In fact, Morgan's "bank" of precise description suggested the idea of inserting other materials into Chainbreaker's story. All quotations from Morgan are drawn from this volume.

Parker, Arthur C. *Seneca Myths and Folk Tales.* Buffalo, NY: Buffalo Historical Society, 1923.

This is the source of the story of "Gononkgoes, the Big Breast."

James E. Seaver, *A Narrative of the Life of Mrs. Mary Jemison.* 1824; reprinted with introduction by June Namias. Norman, OK: University of Oklahoma Press, 1992.

All comments of Mary Jemison derive from this volume. The fame of her narrative is warranted and surely results from Jemison's always specific and colorful description. This must reflect her own language as well as the editor Seaver's skill.

Wallace, Anthony. *The Death and Rebirth of the Seneca.* New York, NY: Vintage, 1972.

This volume, which contains a very full description of post-Revolutionary War events, provided James Duane's comment on suppressing Iroquois identity. Wallace's work resembles Graymont's in being a very rich, detailed and sympathetic account of Native American experience. The *Chainbreaker's War* afterword pays tribute to his thesis that Seneca society "died" in the 1790s and commenced a "rebirth" with the teachings of Handsome Lake.

Walton, William. *A narrative of the captivity and sufferings of Benjamin Gilbert and his family. Who were surprised by the Indians and taken from their farm, on Mahoning creek, in Penn township, Northampton county, not far from where Fort Allen was built, on the frontier of Pennsylvania, in the spring of 1780 . . .* Lancaster, PA: Privately printed, 1890.

Different chapters of this volume give the accounts of different family members. Elizabeth Gilbert's memory of John Huston/Hudson is drawn from her chapter, "Narrative of Elizabeth Gilbert Jr," and Abner Gilbert's memory of Huston/Hudson from the "Account of Abner Gilbert's Captivity."

Wisconsin Historical Society, Madison, WI. Draper Manuscripts. Series F, nos. 16 & 17; Series S, no. 4.

In 1848–1849, Hah Na I Sah or Benjamin Williams sold his transcription of Chainbreaker's narrative to the historian and collector, Lyman Draper. This narrative appears in Series F, no. 16, of the Draper Manuscripts. In 1850, Draper visited the Cattaraugus County Reservation in order to interview Chainbreaker himself. Draper's interview notes, found in his Series S, no. 4, have none of the charm or appeal of the narrative recorded by Hah Na I Sah; Draper sought answers to questions concerning specific military engagements, and he set down Chainbreaker's answers in his own (Draper's) dry words. Hah Na I Sah corresponded with Draper over a period of years after the sale, asking rather forlornly, year after year, about the manuscript and Draper's progress in preparing it for publication. (These letters are also contained in Series F, no. 16.) But Draper collected far more material than he could ever digest or publish, and Chainbreaker's story simply remained in his vast collection of papers dealing with pioneer times in the East and Midwest. Eventually, Draper bequeathed his collection to the State Historical Society of Wisconsin, where he worked from 1854 until his death in 1891.

The interesting statements of Captain John Decker, Jesse McQuigg, and Jane Strope Whitaker all appear in Draper's Series F, no. 17. Hah Na I Sah evidently recorded Decker's memories; Draper copied Strope Whitaker's from a published source, and possibly also copied McQuigg's statement from another published or unpublished source.

Wyoming Historical and Geological Society. *The massacre of Wyoming. The acts of Congress for the defense of the Wyoming Valley, Pennsylvania, 1776-1778: with the petitions of the sufferers by the massacre of July 3, 1778, for congressional aid.* Wilkes-Barre, PA: Printed for the Society, 1895.

The source of excerpts from the petitions of George Ransom, Bertha Jenkins, Elisha Harding, and Ishmael Bennett, all made in 1837.

_____. *Red Jacket Microform* (Transactions of the Buffalo Historical Society). Buffalo, NY: Published by order of the Society, 1885.

This microform, which preserves an early bulletin of the Buffalo

Historical Society, contains within its Appendix No. 19 "A Glimpse of Red Jacket's Family and Tribesmen in 1794, at the Memorable Council at Canandaigua." This page-long item is an extract from the first volume of the diary of Quaker William Savary (in 1885 held by the Friends' Library, Philadelphia, PA). A portion of the extract forms the "epilogue" to Chainbreaker's narrative.

# INDEX

Albany, 42, 48, 70, 71, 174
   council, 40–46, 48
Allegany Reservation, 11
Allegheny River, 30, 36, 95, 131,
   148, 154, 170, 202
   battle at, 98–101
Americans, negotiations with
   Indians, 33–39, 41–46,
   142–155, 158–174

Battles
   Allegheny River, 98–101, 202
   Conesus Lake, 96–97
   Fort Gah Doh Ga, 71–72
   Fort Stanwix, 64–69
   Genesee River, 73–80
   Newtown, 95
   Wyalusing, 81, 88–94
   Wyoming, 26–27, 54, 81,
     82–89, 98
Beatty, Lieutenant Erkuries, 106
Bennett, Ishmael, 87
Big Beaver Creek, 202
Big Sandy Creek, 36, 156
Blacksnake. See Chainbreaker
Bowie, Jim, 54
Boyd, Lieutenant William, 98,
   123
Brant, Joseph, 25, 27, 32, 63, 81,
   88, 89, 94, 120, 130
   against alliance with
     Americans, 40
   meetings with British, 54–56,
     60–62, 149–151
   on settlements in Canada,
     150–151
   and treaty negotiations with
     Americans, 144–146,

   179–184
   at Fort Niagara, 96, 105
   at intertribal peace council,
     193–196
   expedition to western
     Indians, 201
British, negotiations with
   Indians, 49–62, 103–110,
   149–151
Brodhead, Colonel Daniel, 95,
   100, 102, 106
Broken Straw, 98
Buffalo, 153, 154, 198, 200, 207
Buffalo Creek, 110–111, 148,
   172, 174
Burgoyne, General John, 48, 70,
   119
Burnt House, 100
Butler, Captain Walter. See
   Duckey, General
Butler, Colonel John, 58, 66, 81,
   82, 98, 123
Butler, Richard, 162, 167

Canandaigua, 206
Canawagus, 23, 26, 28, 31,
   32–34, 40–41, 87, 103, 112,
   118
Cannonwango Creek, 100, 170
Cass, Captain Jonathan, 184
Cattaraugus County, 154
Cattaraugus Reservation, 11,
   207
Cayuga Indians, 9, 29, 30, 41,
   70, 150, 153, 174, 179
Cayuga Lake, 26, 32, 181
Chainbreaker, 9–10, 11, 31, 63
   after Revolution, 206–208

Conesus Lake battle, 96–97
courtship foiled, 187–190
decorated by George
    Washington, 173–174
deer hunting by, 46
dictation of memoirs, 19–28
encounters with Delaware
    Indians, 131–134, 203–205
expedition to western
    Indians, 200–205
Fort Gah Doh Ga attack,
    71–72
Fort Niagara council,
    103–108
Fort Stanwix battle, 64–69
Fort Stanwix treaty, 141–149
at Genesee Falls, 73–80
grammar and syntax used by,
    22–28
historicity of account, 23–27
meetings with Americans,
    36–39, 40–46, 142–155,
    158–174, 179–184
meetings with British, 49
at Mount Morris, 98
new clothing for, 164
origin of name, 25
portrait painted, 114–115,
    157–158, 166
War of 1812, 207
Wyalusing battle, 88–94
Wyoming battle, 82–87
Cherry Valley, 26, 27
Chesapeake, 48
Chippewa Indians, 150, 192, 193
Cold Spring, 19, 102–103, 207
Conesus Lake, battle at, 96–97, 99
Cornplanter, 22, 25–27, 31, 32,
    33–34, 42, 59, 63, 71
    after Revolution, 206–208

encounter with Delaware
    Indians, 131–134
expedition to western
    Indians, 199, 201
Fort Niagara council,
    103–108
Fort Stanwix treaty, 141–149
meetings with Americans, 36,
    142–155, 158–174, 179–184
meetings with British, 49–56,
    60–61, 110–111
new clothing for, 164
portrait painted, 116,
    157–158, 166
Wyalusing battle, 88–89, 94
Cornplanter's Reservation, 100
Crouse, Peter, 25

Dahgr Yan Doh (Chainbreaker),
    26, 32
Decker, John, 43, 201
Deganawida, 29, 39
Delaware Indians, 20, 40, 88–94,
    100, 131–139, 150,
    162–164, 204
Dickinson, Joseph, 158–166
Draper, Lyman, 23–24, 25, 26,
    108, 208
Duane, James, 140–141
Duckey, General, 82, 86, 87, 88,
    89

Erie, 34, 155, 176, 198, 142

Farmer's Brother, 176, 205
Finger Lakes, 95
Five Nations, 30, 39, 60, 90, 149
Food, burial of, 102–103
Fort Gah Doh Ga, battle at,
    71–72

Fort Niagara, 23, 58–59, 81, 88, 109–111, 145, 147, 151
   council, 96, 103–108
Fort Stanwix, 22, 44, 48, 54, 62, 64–69, 71, 105, 108,
   treaty of, 140–149, 175
Franklin, 202
Franklin Creek, 198
French Creek, 36, 156, 202

Ganondagan, 17–18
Genesee Falls, 72–80
Genesee River, 29–30, 32, 40, 47, 73, 87, 96, 98–99, 103–104, 148, 150, 154
Geneseo, 98
German Flats, 24, 48
Gilbert, Abner, 138
Gilbert, Elizabeth, 133
Gr Go Da Nr Yeh, 179
Grand River, 151
Grant Island, 148

Hah Na I Sah (translator of Chainbreaker's memoirs), 19–26, 206, 208
Handsome Lake, 206–207
Harding, Elisha, 86
Harrisburg, 162
Hartley, Colonel Thomas, 81, 93
He-Who-Skims-the-Floating-Grease, 25
Hiawatha, 29
Howe, General William, 48, 70
Hr De Ga, 134
Hudson, Captain John, 23–24, 27, 188–189
   rescues prisoner from Delaware Indians, 131–139, 163–164

Hudson River, 48
Hunting, 46, 203

Indian languages, diversity and interpretation of, 191–192
Intertribal peace council, 191–196
Iroquois Confederacy, 29–31, 39, 60, 70, 175–195. *See also* Six Nations

Jemison, Mary, 11, 28, 38, 47, 53, 59, 64, 74, 97, 99, 103, 110–111, 131, 171, 189
Jenkins, Bertha, 84
Johnson, Sir John, 130
Johnson, Sir William, 24, 40, 44, 63, 130
Jones, Horatio, 77, 150, 170

Kickapoo Indians, 150, 192, 193, 196–198
King (George III), 19, 37–38, 43–46, 51–57, 60–61, 107, 144, 146
Kittanning, 131

Lake Champlain, 48
Lake Chautauqua, 170–172
Lake Erie, 30, 34, 142, 169, 170, 172, 201
Lake Huron, 169
Lake Ontario, 48–49, 53, 142, 150
Lake Superior, 142, 169
Lewiston, 153
Little Beard, 25
Little Muskingum River, 185
Lytle, Eleanor, 160

Mahoning, 131
Maumee River, 197, 199
McQuigg, Jesse, 45, 142, 181
Miami Indians, 150
Midville, 36, 156, 198
Mohawk Indians, 9, 29, 30, 70, 95, 150, 152–153, 179, 193
Mohawk River, 48, 69, 71, 95, 130
Monongahela River, 39, 185
Morgan, Lewis Henry, 32, 35, 37, 43, 57–58, 72–73, 77, 88, 103, 109, 153–155, 182, 191, 194, 197
Morris, Thomas, 180
Mount Morris, 98

New York, 9, 11, 29, 81, 95, 153–154, 157, 166–167, 170
Newtown, battle at, 95
Niagara Falls, 58, 105, 153
Niagara River, 148, 151, 168–169

O'Bail, John. See Cornplanter
Ohio River, 175
Oil Springs Reserve, 11, 208
Old Smoke (Young King), 63
Olean Creek, 148
Oneida Indians, 9, 29, 30, 70, 97, 98, 108–109, 111, 141, 146, 150, 154
Onondaga Indians, 9, 27, 29, 30, 47, 95, 150, 154, 177, 179
  neutrality in war, 70, 105, 106–107
Oriskany, 24, 28, 66, 70, 120
Osage Indians, 24, 26, 185–191, 192, 193. See also Shawnee Indians
Oswego, 25, 63

Parker, Arthur C., 104, 136, 187, 190, 193
Pennsylvania, 9, 26, 29, 81, 170
Philadelphia, 48, 70, 126, 133, 157, 160, 166, 175–184
Pittsburgh, 100, 133, 139, 157, 158, 177, 182
  council at, 23, 43, 33–40, 48
Pollard, Captain, 88–89
Potawatomi Indians, 150, 192, 193
Potter, Brigadier General James, 81, 90–93
Prisoner, rescued from Delaware Indians, 131–139, 162–164

Ransom, George, 84, 86
Red Eyes, 98–101, 102–103
Red Jacket, 21, 25, 27, 31, 32, 33, 40, 103, 128, 190, 196
  Chainbreaker's opinion of, 207–208
  Fort Stanwix treaty, 141–149
  intertribal peace council, 193
  meetings with Americans, 36–38, 44–45, 155, 173, 179–184
  meetings with British, 51, 54–56
  new clothing for, 164
  Wyalusing battle, 88–89, 94

Sandusky, 153
Saratoga, 70
Savary, William, 205
Schoharie River, 130
Schuyler, Colonel Philip, 41
Seneca Indians, 9–12, 16–19, 29–32, 41–46, 68, 70, 81, 95, 124, 130–134, 150, 153
  after Revolution, 206–208

Seneca Lake, 26, 29, 30, 96
Shawnee Indians, 26, 150,
    189–191
Simmons, Henry, Jr., 182
Six Nations, 9, 30, 31, 37, 39–46,
    61–62, 96–98, 140–141,
    193. *See also* Iroquois
    Confederacy
  dispersal over United States
    and Canada, 152–154
  expedition to western
    Indians, 200–204
  Fort Niagara council,
    103–108
  Fort Stanwix treaty discus-
    sion, 149
  meetings with Americans,
    142–155
  meetings with British, 49–62,
    109–110
  settlement at Buffalo Creek,
    110–111
  war with Americans contin-
    ued, 154–155
  Wyalusing battle, 88–94
Solato River, 198
So No So Wa, 31, 63
St. Leger, Colonel Barry, 48, 70
Strong, Captain, 131–134,
    179–184
Sullivan, Major General John,
    95, 98, 99, 110, 121, 124,
    171, 184, 185
Susquehanna River, 88, 95

Tallchief, Emily, 199

Tan Wyr Nyrs, 9, 19, 25, 31, 32.
    *See also* Chainbreaker
Thayendanegea. *See* Brant,
    Joseph
Thirteen Nations, 150–151, 193
Trumbull, Jonathan, 157
Tuscarora Indians, 9, 30, 70, 150,
    153, 177, 179

Upper Sandusky River, 202
Utica, 153

Van Campen, Major Moses, 46

War of 1812, 207
Warren County, 99, 103
Washington, George, 24, 32, 43,
    46, 95, 107, 108, 127, 128,
    141, 145–155, 157–174,
    175–184, 194–195, 200
West, Benjamin, 157
Western Indians, 175–198,
    199–204
Whitaker, Jane Strope, 63, 73,
    83, 145, 146, 186, 191
Williams, Benjamin. *See* Hah
    Na I Sah
Wyalusing, 27
  battle at, 81, 88–94
Wyandot Indians, 150, 191, 193
Wyoming, battle at, 26–27, 81,
    82–90, 98

Young King, 63, 88–89, 94, 149,
    155, 164, 179